My Soul Cries Out

Inspirational Journal

By Phyllis S. Gates

My Soul Cries Out

Inspiration Journal

Written by Phyllis S. Gates

Table of Contents

Trails and Treasure   5

Seasons   7

Whale Diaries   21

Freedom Song   35

Abiding   49

Teach Us To Pray   67

Higher Ground   79

Wings   91

Celebrate   103

With Unveiled Face   115

Then Sings My Soul   127

Light   141

Trails and Treasures

I love to paint pictures, especially pictures of the local landscape. Continually amazed at its beauty, from the majestic mountain peaks, orchard blossoms, and the seemingly never ending rows of crops preparing for harvest.

Sitting in the stillness of my writing chair, my ear catches the sounds of song birds, invading my yard at spring time. From the golden finch that adds such color and life to the often gray skies of the Northwest, to the golden vineyards of fall, each season has its own delights.

My mind takes a journey with my pioneer ancestors who ventured across unmapped territory reaching the crest of rocky plains and gazing upon endless miles of virgin territory. Over the years sights have transformed from wide open ranges, endless starlit skies, to the lights of city splendor, bridges stretching across continuing waterways of imagination.

The heart's desire presses us to venture into new territory for good intention. Dreams and vision plow the roads forward, as we look now to the heavens for even greater adventure. We are struck with ever increasing wonders, light years of new uncharted space, visions of nebulas, light echoes, and increasing galaxies.   The pioneer spirit pushes onward to greater knowledge and understanding, as the sound of outer space creates an unending praise to its creator.

How big does it get, how far can we go? Will all the questions ever all be answered?

With dreams born in God's own heart, imparted in us for greatness, destiny and purpose, determined for all mankind, the mystery presses us onward and deeper, to know all there is to know.

Created in the deepest recesses of man's heart is a territory that God wants to possess. Amidst the noise of modern life, we can venture into that place where the throne of the Living God abides. He speaks to our awaiting souls, imparting revelation, mysteries of ages past, present and future. We are wise to explore the inner territory of our soul.

Seasons

A Time for Every Reason
From Psalm 23

Introduction

Seasons are part of the mystery of life. We all experience them, but why must we go through such times? Is there some divine destination that can only be reached by the challenges and victories that each season brings?

We are all on our own individual journeys, passing through seasons of life, and there is an eternal purpose for each of the paths we travel. We encounter sojourners on the way, and we have opportunity to encourage the wayward soul. We are likewise guided down the road by those who have traversed the territory before us.

Deliberately choose life, not passively in a ho-hum way, but with determination that today is a gift from God. Whether through highs or lows, God is with you and you will see His goodness in the land of the living.

Life is a journey of the soul, with a beginning and a destination, and the roads we choose make all the difference in where we end up, for eternity.

New Beginnings

We were blessed with the birth of a new granddaughter today, and I contemplate the newness of her life. What a wonder, so fresh, so tender, no guile, no fear, cradled in the safety of her father's arms.

Oh, to recapture that fresh springtime innocence of the soul, the new birth, hold on to it with all its potential and freedom, and the grace of being completely forgiven and set free.

Like a newborn babe, the spirit is born and liberated from the confines of a darkened soul, a new creation in Christ. Behold, all things are new. We look into our Father's eyes, face to face He holds us.

Life so full of promise, the Father's heart can hardly wait to show us off. Patiently He waits, watching our steps of growth, picking us up when we fall, and setting our feet on a firm foundation. He promises that nothing can ever separate us from His love.

"Fear not little one, for I am with you always", He assures us.

"THE LORD is my shepherd; I shall not want."

Learning to Lean

A child trusts in his parents to provide for his every need. Even in the most dire of circumstances, a child of lowly estate has confidence that he is provided for, and he does not fret nor worry.

Parents are only human. We make mistakes leaving wounds and scars. But as one who is born of the Spirit, we can have an abiding confidence that God sees us, he knows our deepest and most personal needs, both physical and spiritual. In the richness and goodness of creation, God left nothing out of His lavish resources for us, both for life and godliness.

If we ask our earthly father for a loaf of bread, will he give a stone? Of course not. How much more then will our Heavenly Father give to us who ask? The Holy Spirit will teach us and bring to our remembrance all things, and He will guide us to unexpected resources.

Our Heavenly Father delights in pouring out blessings upon us. All good things come from His hand.

"Ask and you will be given, seek and you will find, knock and the door will be opened," Jesus said, doors to great revelation into the storehouse of spiritual mystery and wonders.

"He makes me to lie down in green pastures"

Peace

In a world of chaos, it is sometimes difficult to find a place of peace, a tranquil spot of rest where the clatter and the hustle bustle world is far away. We search for such a place and pay big money when we can find it.

Even Jesus regularly went to His certain place, to draw away from the crowds. That is where He could most clearly hear the voice of the Father. We all need a place like that, be it aboard our boat, a cabin by the lake, or a special chair right in our own home. It is a place where we wait upon God. We listen, we pray, we draw near, we get to know Him intimately. Here we can tune out the world, approach His heart and to seek His face. That is our place of peace.

There is as well a place deep within our soul, where at a moment's notice we can draw into, amidst a crowded mall or walking on a populated beachfront. It is a place of His presence.

Jesus said, "draw near to me, and I will draw near to you."

As we find Him there in that place, we will continually be drawn back, whatever the cost.

"He leads me beside the still waters.
He restores my soul."

Fruit Bearing

There was a time when we had a large number of fruit trees on our property. There was bounty of every kind. The trees took a lot of work to keep them bearing a good crop, though. The sunlight had to be adequate, the temperature warm enough, the watering just so, and the pruning most critical. There was one apple tree that just didn't seem to do well. The apples were few, small and sour. Otherwise, the tree was beautifully full and leafy, but looks were deceiving.

One night we had an especially strong storm and when we checked on the trees in the morning, that apple tree was laying flat on the ground, exposing a shallow inadequate root system. It became evident that all its growing was going to the showy leaves and branches up on top.

Fruit trees must be cut way back at just the right time to allow a good crop of fruit in its season. It is all about the roots and the fruit. Otherwise, the tree is merely for show, and it will eventually fall.

God knows when our pruning is needed most. It is for our good, as good fruit is vital to the Kingdom of God, as we represent the King. We are His ambassadors, and our lives affect the souls of many, and how they see God.

"He leads me in the paths of righteousness
for His name's sake."

Storms

As we sojourn through this life on earth, we will occasionally pass through rocky waters, not easily navigated. Those are the times in our lives that shape us and define who we are and who we will become.

We had such a time in our life. Our six year old grandson was diagnosed with a cancerous tumor in his spinal cord. The doctors gave him a few painful weeks to survive and predicted that when he eventually entered a coma, it would be a blessing. That time of our life reduced us to our very core. It would reveal the truth about who we were and what we stood for.

We were lost in a storm of life. There were no doctors anywhere who would take his case, or offer any new hope. Our only hope could be found in God alone, so that is where we went.   It was our deepest valley, but God was there. Through it we discovered all the resources God could provide, including great emboldened faith, comfort and peace beyond our human understanding, and eventually unexpected provisions and unexplainable miracles of healing.

We learned that no mountain is too high or valley too deep that God is not there in the midst guiding us to the other side.

"Yea, though I walk through the valley of the shadow of death, I will fear no evil, for You are with me."

Mountain Tops

Mountains are exhilarating to look upon. They reveal proper perspective and make one dream of flying like a bird to see the world from God's point of view. Sometimes mountains must be conquered, and it appears daunting and impossible. How can I ever overtake this mountain in my life, we ask? It is accomplished like everything else, one step at a time. Taking the first step is the bravest and most important of all.

We all have mountains of different names in our lives, so we can never judge another person's mountain. We climb our individual peaks at different paces, cheering each other on as we go. On our journey we encounter beasts and jagged edges, narrow passages and steep rocks. Someone to hold on to can save us from certain death. That is how the shepherd guides the sheep up to the high places. He has a rod to guide the sheep along and a staff to grab onto them, sometimes called a goad. "It hurts to kick against the goad," Jesus said, so the sheep comply to the discipline of it. They trust their lives in the hand of the shepherd.

The Lord Himself is our Shepherd and we can have confidence and peace that there is no mountain too high, and He will guide us to safety and victory.

"Your rod and Your staff, they comfort me."

Seed Time and Harvest

The spring rains have come and gone. The furrows are broken up and the seed is in the ground. It has been a long hot summer, the work has been hard and exhausting. The elements seemed to be working against us so much of the time, with blight, locusts, drought. Will this season ever end, and will the rain ever fall again?

Early in the morning to late at night, the work of the field must press on, two steps forward and one step back. Persevering under tremendous opposition and pressure, we watch and pray for the late rains to soften the soil.

Then one autumn morning we gaze upon the acres of our labor and see. The fields are ripe and ready for harvest, as far as the eye can see. It is harvest time, and the work seems to have just begun.

Pray to the Lord of the Harvest that He send the laborers into the field. The harvest is so abundant that one cannot handle it alone, so the workers unite together for the common cause our differences seem so petty now. The harvest has come and the gates of hell cannot prevail against it. It is time for celebration.

*"You prepare a table before me in
the presence of my enemies."*

Deep Cries Unto Deep

The longing heart knows. There is more. I cannot, I must not be satisfied. There is more to see, there is more to do, there is more to understand. So, I step out into deeper waters, ankle deep to knee deep, I venture in.

From glory to glory, the current carries me, from knee deep to waist deep. Still, my longing soul yearns, as long as my feet touch the soil below, I have not experienced the deepest demands of my aching heart. I take the plunge, I dive to depths I cannot master in my own power or ability.

Come Holy Spirit, take me where no man can manage, where I must trust in the assurance of Your power and strength to carry me. Take me on to the depths of the sea, to the place of miracles, signs and wonders. Empower me by Your Spirit, enable me to do those greater things which you spoke of.

God awaits only for my willingness, the expectant determination to jump in head first. The skies of heaven are open, the latter rain is here and I must go where the current takes me.

"You anoint my head with oil; My cup runs over."

Life is Good

Some days are like that. Life is a beach. The sun is shining, the clouds are few, and the wind is warm and gentle. The kites are soaring high, and the goodness of God just seems overwhelming to all our senses. These are days of rest, days of reflection and thanksgiving.

"God has been good to me," my heart proclaims.

It is a time to notice the little things, the footprints in the sand of those who have prepared the way before, to smell the freshness of the ocean breeze, to sit and restore strength for the days to come. It is a time to reflect on the abiding love of God, seeing Him as He always is. Even on those days when life is demanding, and we are too busy to notice, His waves of mercy never ending.

God gives such days of rest, and we are to take them without guilt or condemnation, for indeed He created them and said it was good. Essential for our spiritual health, we contemplate the hand of God, His grace and favor going before us and His love and mercy following behind, working all things for our good.

*"Surely goodness and mercy shall follow
me all the days of my life,"*

Twilight

There comes a season in life when we are at peace in the knowledge that the work is accomplished. Oh, there is always more to do, but it comes as a bonus. We know that God is not finished with us yet, but we rest in the reality that our life is in its twilight time. We are totally at peace with it. The thought of death has lost its sting.

A heart becomes almost homesick as a child longs to again see the faces of parents and grandparents. Sometimes it is a child who has gone on before and we long for the day we will embrace them again. Knowing that they all will be there waiting to welcome us in makes the crossing a distant delight.

In the quietness of moments, under the star lit heavens, one can almost hear the wedding preparations in progress. Angelic bridal attendants stand at attention, in anticipation of the moment when we are escorted to the Bridegroom's side. The beckoning is nearly irresistible.

"And I will dwell in the house of the
LORD Forever."

The Meantime

What we do in the meantime can make all the difference. The fact is, it's not over till it's over, and while we look forward to eternity we must occupy. God has created each of us with a purpose beyond our comprehension. From the time of our youth we search, we wonder and prepare.

Our culture too often wrongly assumes that our life purpose is somehow fulfilled in our youthful years. God sees the beginning from the end, and it is often in our elder years that God's purposes in our life all make sense. We will see life as a beautiful tapestry of events, all fitting together for our very best.

The future is something we see from afar off dimly, like a road that stretches far into the horizon at sunset. Yet, we see clearly the road set immediately before us ultimately reaching the destination of a lifetime. It is good to hear the counsel and experiences of those who have set the course before us. They have seen the pot holes and surprises that life can bring.

The road has been traveled most of the way, and the end is coming into focus. We see how the artistry has woven together to reveal the purposes of our combined destinies. We are determined to finish the race strong, yearning to hear those words, "well done, My good and faithful friend."

My Thoughts and Prayers

Whale Diaries

Life in the Spirit

Setting Sail

A few years back, my husband and I were invited on a sailing trip that changed my personal perspective on many levels. At the time, I was recovering from some physical illness and disappointments. My mind was very focused on my needs. How often we allow ourselves to take the preeminent place in our life. Everything comes down to my health, my feelings, and my discomfort. We begin to see life through the pinhole of our own existence, and it was at such a time in my life.

As we set out on the open waters of the San Juan Islands, the quiet hum of the motor and the splashing of the water on the sides of the boat were all the sounds we could hear. It seemed to drown out all the clatter of life that we had left behind. No internet, no radio and no newspapers to divert our attention back to life in our world.

One of the goals of our traveling party was to journal the still small voice of God during our days, to fully absorb His still small voice. Faced with the grandeur of creation, my first reminder was of the smallness of man in comparison. As God and I got that point settled, He began to speak to my heart from a higher perspective.

"What is man that thou art mindful of him," was a question I asked.

God's answers are amazing. He is delighted to fill you in.

Then They Came

Each day of our journey, I whispered a simple prayer. "Send the whales Lord, what a blessing it would be to see the whales today."

The last full day of the journey, my vigil I continued. "It would sure be amazing to see the whales before we go home."

At the end of the trip, still no whales were seen. Our prayers can be like that. God always hears our prayers, but sometimes, as it was with the whales, it is the next group of travelers, the next generation that reaps the rewards of those prayers.

In the still waters of a lukewarm church, our hearts cry out for revival. Year after year the prophets proclaim, "it's coming, it's on it way, it's just around the corner." Our hearts are hopeful, maybe this is the year. In time we see the stirring of the waters. Life becomes increasingly rocky, but our spirits continue, "Even so, come Lord Jesus." We know something is just below the surface edge. We can smell it like a summer rain creeping across a dry dusty field.

In the faithfulness of God, proving the value of prayer, the waters burst forth with life, and all of creation, as if dancing before the Lord, breaks forth with singing. The exquisite creatures of the deep arising in all their splendor to join the chorus. The power of prayer is never lost, but carries forth for generations to come.

It Was Good

The news on the TV and internet make it sound like the planet is spinning out of control, ready to collapse upon itself at any moment. Back on the mainland, there seems to be no way to escape, minds and hearts grows weary from all the pressures and negative messages. We must simply draw away from time to time.

There is nothing like getting out into nature that puts life in perspective. It reminds us that there is still a God who sees from Heaven, and we are the sheep of His hand. The birds of the air, the beasts of the land and sea rest in the sovereignty of God. They neither toil nor worry, but gather the fruits of their bounty without concern for tomorrow. That is rest at its best.

God created the heavens and the earth to be a blessing to man and beast alike. The beauty and abundance of nature is where we see how it was meant to be. The rich harvest of the land is enjoyed by all, with rejoicing in the truth that it is indeed good.

Enjoying the Journey

Just as God chose us in Him before the foundation of the world, inviting us to join Him on a fabulous journey called life. Some mornings we awaken to still and calm waters, the tide is out and we feel the gentle breeze of peace. Some days are embraced by the wind and full of power, if we are brave enough to unfurl the sails. Some days are covered with clouds and rain. We batten down the hatches, draw in together and patiently find joy the fellowship of friends and family.

"Be still and know that I am God", scripture says. Sit down with a hot cup of coffee, His word and enjoy the ride. Marvel at His creation, those things that reveal His glory and abundance.

When the waters are stormy, keep focus on what you know to be true rather than feelings, which can be deceiving. The instruments will guide even when fog envelopes the landscape. Let faith lead your heart, knowing that you will see the goodness of God in the land of the living.

Turning Points

Life is full of turning points, although not always clearly marked and easy to recognize. It is never too late to turn around and choose a new course of direction.

To repent, we have been told, is to turn one-hundred-eighty degrees and go back the other way. It actually means to re-pent, to return to the pentacle, the higher ground from which you fell.

To continue in a wrong direction can be heavy and burdensome, but when we spy a spot in the road of life, a place to make a U turn, and we make the brave decision to take it. The turning point becomes the place where you lay down the heavy load. It is a place of obedience and a place of trust, a rest stop for a weary soul. It can also become a place of excitement and anticipation of what lies ahead. Our decisions to obey are never overlooked by God.

Signs and Wonders

While sitting on the boat, enjoying the evening sunset, we were captivated by a remarkable image on the horizon. A spot of rainbow sat just above the setting sun. There was no beginning and no end, only a spot. Our cameras were all focused, snapping to capture the moment. It was not until later as we enjoyed the photos that the two eagle clouds soaring overhead caught our attention. One was a full eagle's head, the other of an eagle soaring with wings extend from north to south.

God had been reminding us that as we wait upon Him, our strength would be restored and we would fly with eagle's wings. That is what signs and wonders are supposed to do, capture our attention and cause us to take notice.

Man needs signs along the way, signs that say, "stop, listen, God is saying something in your midst." Not always dramatic, signs will teach us and reveal important things, often revelations for those who have eyes to see and ears to hear.

We are instructed that God will reveal times and seasons by signs. Pay attention, look up, they warn. The heavens and prophets let us know, the time is at hand.

"They that wait upon the Lord will renew their strength. They will mount up with wings like the eagles." Isaiah 40:31

Waiting

There are times in life when our hearts, minds and spirits grow weary. From overwork, illness or disappointment, such is common to man. Weariness does not mean weakness though. Adversity can make you grow or it can do you in, depending on our attitude, turning us into an eagle, heaven bound, or into a chicken, confined to the ground. What we do in the midst of adversity is what counts.

It is not how we fall that counts, but how we get up. Do I depend on my own resources or cry out for God's, limitless in power and strength? God says to wait upon Him.

To wait, however, does not mean to passively sit back, allowing time to be wasted. It is not passive at all, but rather aggressive. We actively choose to draw close, to pray, to listen and partake of His presence, and as we do, His strength restores us.

The eagle embraces the storm, and soars on the wings of the wind. In our waiting, we are infused by resurrection power that lifts us up where we will soar in the midst of challenge.

Isaiah 40:29, "He gives power to the faithful; and to them that have not might, he increases strength. "

Sailing

Life is a lot like sailing. We can choose to drop anchor and stay in shallow waters, or we can pull it up and begin our journey. The choices continue, as we can run under the predictability of engine power, or unfurl the sails and let the power of the wind take us where it wants to go.

With wisdom and discernment, the experienced sailor can guide the craft, watching the movement of the wind and stirring of deep waters. It takes confidence to turn off the engine and open up the sails.

Our confidence is in God. When the Spirit is given permission to take control, the journey becomes powerful, sometimes turbulent, sometimes quiet, never dull, and always unpredictable. One must be vigilant, disciplined, watching, preparing, and being ready in season and out.

Enjoy the sunny blue skies and clear waters while you may, because the power of the wind comes with clouds and storm, trials and testing. As the storm clouds rise and the winds bear down, it is time to open up the sails and see where the Spirit will take us.

All hands on deck, listening and watching the commands of the Captain, He watches the tell tale signs and familiar landmarks to stay on course, because it is time for the ride of your life.

Sleeping Through the Storm

One afternoon I was feeling a bit sleepy. The winds were sleepy also and we were running on light engine power, so I decided to take opportunity to slip down below and catch some rest.

No sooner had I crawled into the berth, the breezes began to stir, quickly growing to a gale, and then very strong winds. The boat rocked to and fro and up and down. I had to position my feet against the side walls not to be tossed around.

Above, I could hear the unfurling of the sails and the ropes slapping the sides of the boat. Taking advantage of the power of the wind, sailing got underway,.

Funny thing happened down below. I fell asleep in the storm without so much as an anxious thought. I knew the ship was in the experienced hands of a master skipper. Later, when I woke up, the winds were stilled, and the waters calm. We had passed through the storm.

Life is very much like that. One does not linger in a storm with the anchor dropped. Storms come to pass, and this one too shall pass. The quality of our rest is determined by our confidence in the One who is at the helm.

Rock Solid

From John's gospel, we learn that the Word was with God from the beginning of creation, and the Word was God. The Word became flesh and dwelt among us, and we beheld His glory, as of the only Begotten Son.

Jesus, He is the Solid Rock, the revelation on which we stand and build every good work. Our foundation, our cornerstone and capstone, He is the beginning and the end.

Sailing through the channels of open water, one can see giant rock formations, high above the water's edge. They are landmarks, familiar and reliable. The sailor can count on them to guide the journey start to finish.

The word of God, inspired and true, is our rock solid and reliable. We can stand on it and we can trust it to bear the full weight of truth. Considering the entire council of God's word, we can put our complete confidence upon it. God's word is truth, and knowing it will change our perspective on everything.

Renewal

Every good tale has a beginning and it has an ending. Like the journey of life, we are either at one end or the other, or somewhere in between. To be called to such a journey as this was beyond wonderful, deserving of a thankful heart.

As I consider my life, a speck of time in the grand providence of God, I am amazed by His grace and purpose. Looking upon the generations past and future, my hope is restored. Can God's grace be promised any less to my children than what I have experienced? Certainly not.

As I approached this journey's end, I am left with renewed strength to press onward, to finish the race strong, yet with a sense that I have just begun. In God's economy, all endings are but a transition to new beginnings starting today and forever.

My Thoughts and Prayers

Freedom Song

From Psalm 103

Knowing

It was always confusing to me, the verse in Matthew, chapter 25, "To him who has, more will be given, but to him who has not, even what he has will be taken away".

Clearly, all of us have been given many blessings. We can have forgiveness, righteousness, grace, favor, everything that pertains to life and godliness. That is what Scripture tells us. Experiencing must include the matter of knowing and believing. We can have a treasure stored away for us, but if we don't know it or we don't believe it, then it will do us no benefit. What we have is robbed from us by our own lack of understanding and disbelief.

Psalm 103 tells us to "forget not His benefits", be aware of them, and know them. The key to experiencing the treasure is not a matter of hope, but knowing, believing, and remembering.

When our grandson, Daniel, was given a diagnosis for stage four cancer, a tumor in his spinal cord, the report was devastating, in one word, death. We were getting words from many people, encouraging words, comforting words, words of hope, and even words preparing us for the very worst. This was a time when we were desperate for a word from God. He gave us Psalm 103. We read it, shared it, and posted it on the refrigerator. Faith began to rise up with a deep knowing that God said what He meant and meant what He said. God not only said it but He told us not to forget it.

What's In A Name

Jesus, the name that is above every name, is the Light in a dark and lonely place, to whom every knee will bow.

I enter Your gates with thanksgiving for all that you have done, and I press on to Your courts with praise for who You are. Draw me ever closer to the inner chambers of Your Holy place. With a grateful heart I come, Your hand ever reaching out, I press onward, deeper and deeper, higher and higher, by the increasing Spirit of revelation to understand the heights and depths of Your endless love and kindness.

I marvel at the power of Your name. It would take a lifetime to comprehend the fullness of it. Jesus, You told us in John's Gospel, on the eve of Your crucifixion, that as we are in You and You are in us, we can ask whatsoever we will in Your Name and the Father who is in heaven will do it. Did you really mean to say that? Is that what you really meant to say?

Yes indeed, the Father's heart is touched with our grief and responds to the prayers offered in Your name at the bedside of a dying child. My heart rejoices in awe and amazement at the authority of the Name of Jesus. With all that is within me, I bless Your Holy Name.

"Bless the Lord, Oh my soul, and all that is within me, bless His Holy Name."

Don't Forget

What manner of love is this, that while I was yet in the depths of despair and disrepair, You came for me. Praise shall continually be in my mouth, and I will not forget.

Lifting the cup of communion, I remember. Your body was broken for me and your bloodshed restored me to my God ordained place and purpose, established from eternity past. You bought me back, and reconciled me to a Father's broken heart.

I am not a second hand rose, but a pearl of great price. You gave up everything that Heaven could afford to come to earth and pay the ultimate price. With great pain and sorrow, You redeemed my past, my present and my future. You restored all that the locust had eaten, and the fields are again ripe unto harvest.

Your hand extended with compassion and mercy to a sick child, I will not forget. Let me never forget. I will sing of the mercy of the Lord forever, with my mouth I will make known Thy faithfulness to all generations.

"Bless the Lord, Oh my soul, and forget not all His benefits."

No Condemnation

Jesus, You have shown the Father's love, compassion and grace. Even though I still wrestle with unclean influences of this world, You accomplished Your task, and I am deemed forgiven, set free. You were wounded for my transgression, bruised for my iniquity as You cried from the Cross, "It is finished".

Now I stand before You clean, without spot or wrinkle, the righteousness of God in Christ. Not only did you clean the house, You set up residence and posted signs on the door, "No Trespassing", "Private Property", "Guard On Duty".

You venture deep within my wounded inner man to heal, patching the cracks in the walls, making the abode a fortress. You have become my shield and defender. You restored my broken down habitation and fashioned a high tower, a refuge, a safe place in the storm of life. You watch the walls and warn me of impending breaches that could allow opportunity for the tormentor.

Be it by a cloud or a pillar of fire, You are there. Whether by the still waters and green pastures, or through the shadow of death, You are there. You never leave my side, and all fear is gone. The work you have begun, You will complete. Fan the flame within me, blow away the ashes until that day, when You gaze back at me, You see only the shining reflection of Your glorious image.

"Who forgives all your iniquities."

All Means All

Jesus, on the Cross, You carried my sorrow and pain, and by Your stripes I am healed. It is not a two step program, but an all inclusive package deal, the Gift that keeps on giving. I am a work in progress, step by step, unfolding grace upon grace.

All means all, and nothing less. Beginning the day I first received You into my heart, until the day this earthly bodily house is redeemed in the resurrection, You are in the process of affirming me with, "Yes and Amen!"

There is nothing impossible with You, no disease or cursed thing has any claim. Every name that is named, including cancer and depression, must bow to the Lordship and authority of Your name. You search my heart and know my ways, and as You do, You heal the wounds of the past, and deliver me from plaguing spirits that have sought to destroy me.

You will not save my soul only to leave me to my own resources. I do not need to search for ways to finish what You have done. You are faithful and true to complete the work which You have begun in me. It is for liberty that I have been set free.

"Who healed all your diseases."

Pits are The Pits

Pits come in all sizes and depths, and we can find ourselves in pits for various reasons. Sometimes it is by a life time of poor choices, sometimes a momentary misstep, and sometimes by the misstep of another. Other times pits just happen, because the world we live in is full of them.

Sometimes we will spend a lifetime trying to climb out, only to dig ourselves ever deeper. We conclude that nothing will ever change, so we find comfort in our destructive place. Fashioning a comfy chair, we take a cup of self-pity and wallow in misfortune. Loneliness becomes the hearth of our despairing abode, no one comes to visit there, for it is a sad place, after all.

Do you not know? Have you not heard? Hope arises and the heart looks upward and wonders, is it possible? Take the risk and gaze upward into the light. God's radiance is at the end of the cold dark tunnel, His hand stretching forth. Muster the courage to grab hold, and find yourself standing on higher ground, a sure foundation. Joy fills the air like fragrant blossoms of springtime. The places of destruction become a fading memory, as we fix our gaze on His endless love. He will lift us out of despair and give beauty for ashes, the oil of joy for mourning. In this place of rest, our hearts will join in the song of freedom.

"Who redeems your life from destruction."

Crowns of Glory

As for God's loving kindness and tender mercies, we cannot escape them. They follow endlessly wherever we go, with unmerited and unlimited favor of God. He loves with an everlasting love. "I am His and He is mine," becomes our banner. Resting in the firm grip of His able hands as His watchful eye, He shows Himself strong on our behalf.

His loving kindness is ever guiding us to wellsprings of blessing, His tender mercies intervening to protect us from paths of destruction. Nothing can separate us from His love, neither height nor depth, nor blessing nor persecution.

We cannot minimize the power of our prayers. The Father longs to give all that we need and desire, everything that pertains to life and godliness. We can ask for far greater blessing than we feel worthy of receiving, because God sees us through different eyes than we see ourselves. Even when we see ourselves as unclean and unworthy, He sees us as white like snow, as the righteousness of God in Christ.

As we begin to comprehend who we are in Christ, and all that He has made available to His beloved, it will change our perspective and our relationship with Him. The storehouse of heaven is at our disposal, so we can ask for mighty and amazing things. It is the Father's delight to bless us beyond imagination, more than we can ask or dream.

"Who crowns you with loving kindness and tender mercies."

Strength and Vitality

Nothing was left undone or incomplete. We are forgiven, healed and delivered. If God would send His Son to die for us, how much more will He freely give us all things?

God, You sent Your Holy Spirit to satisfy the longings of our most inner person, and You provided for all our physical needs with good things. Forget not the smallest details, from herbal delights to springs of living water, in You, our youth is renewed like the eagle's.

Fly mighty eagle, be strengthened to rise from ashes of discouragement, to catch the wind and soar above the storm. Stretch your wings and reach the heights of heavenly places. Every gust is but an opportunity for victory, victory upon victory. No storm can overtake you because you sail above the circumstances of life.

Set your feet upon higher ground, the God ordained, eternal destiny for your life, established in eternity past. Higher, higher you will reach. You are a champion. Nothing is impossible with God, and nothing can stop you. Your mouth will proclaim the glory of God, "Oh, magnify the Lord, Oh my soul."

"Who satisfies your mouth with good things so your youth is renewed like the eagle's."

How Deep and Wide

You alone, Oh God, can hold the scales in perfect balance. The weight of sin so mysteriously leveled by Your compassion. You measure the tears of the oppressed in Your hand, and on the other You are not willing that any should perish. Your long suffering is impossible to humanly comprehend.

The mercy of God was set in motion in eternity past with a plan of redemption for sin not yet committed. Oh that God Himself would prepare for the moment of mercy, to be willingly nailed to a cross, the devil's folly and claim over us would be broken once and for all time.

You oh God, became sin for us that we might become Your righteousness. Mercy has overwhelmed transgression. The price paid for our rebellion so costly that no balance due could ever exist. The debt is cleared and it is for freedom that we have been set free.

"For as the heavens are high above the earth,
so great is His mercy toward those who fear Him;"

From Start to Finish

Bless the Lord, who reigns on high. You observe our comings and our goings, and Your righteousness and dominion cover the earth. Angels, countless in number, harkening to Your voice, the bidding of Your command, called forth to serve one blood bought soul.

Life has had its trials, tests to prove your greatness, little one. They have had purpose working all things for your good. You are surrounded by the hosts of heaven to guard you in all your ways. Fear not, He is with you. Wait upon the Lord. Learn and be established in the Word, and listen, as you find that secret place of His presence. Wait aggressively on Him, praying, seeking, drawing ever closer to His heart beat. You will run and not grow weary, and you will walk and not faint.

You were created for such a time as this, mighty warrior. Be the history maker, life changer, as you were created to be. Conquer and take territory for the Kingdom. Your purpose and destiny are limited only by what the mind and heart of God can dream.

God's mercy is from everlasting to everlasting upon His children, and righteousness upon their children's children. Bless the Lord, bless the Lord, Oh my soul.

"The mercy of the Lord is from everlasting to everlasting on those who fear Him, and His righteousness to children's children."

The Story Continues

The years since Daniel was diagnosed with cancer has been a journey that would clarify God's most intimate purpose in our lives, to know Him and the power of His resurrection. God Himself touched Daniel one glorious night, a week before Christmas. Pain endured for the night, but joy came in the morning.

The years have been a tapestry of one God ordained provision after another, orchestrated with such precision that no human could have planned it. Hospitals, surgeons, nurses, airline pilots and teachers, were placed by God's marvelous destiny, positioned at the precise time for such a cause as this.

The appreciation our family has for all these wonderful giving individuals who have touched our lives is inexpressible. The many prayer warriors continue to take up Daniel's cause unceasingly and at a moment's notice.

As a young man now, we have not yet seen the rest of the story, accept through the many visions and dreams of others. One thing we know is that Daniel is a man of destiny, born and prepared for greatness. Our heart's rejoice at all God has done and continues to do. We will not forget, no never.

"Bless the Lord, bless the Lord, Oh my soul."

My Thoughts and Prayers

Abiding

From Gospel of John

"I am the true vine, and My Father is the vinedresser"
"Abide in Me and I in you. As the branch cannot
bear fruit of itself"
"He who abides in Me, and I in him, bears much fruit"
"If you abide in Me, and My words abide in you,
you will ask what you desire, and it shall be done"
"As the Father loved Me, I also have loved you;
abide in My love"
"These things I have spoken to you,
that My joy may remain in you,
and your joy may be full"
"This is My commandment, that you love one another
as I have loved you"
"Greater love has no one that this,
than to lay down one's life for his friends"
"You are My friend, if you do whatever I command you"
"You did not choose Me, but I chose you and appointed you
that you should go and bear fruit,
and that your fruit should remain,
that whatever you ask the Father in My name
He may give you"

From the Gospel of John, Chapter 14

Process

As I look out the windows of our Northwest home, upon the surrounding hillsides I delight in the many vineyards in every direction. In springtime the field crews are cleaning up the vines, washing off the branches soiled from the rains, trimming off excess growth of wild branches.

In the summertime, the lush and green hillsides are alive and thriving. Walking through the rows, we would see the tiny green clusters of new fruit, shining metal strips tied to the vines to deter the birds. This is a wonderful season of anticipation and preparation. It is going to be a good year.

Then comes the autumn, the hillsides aglow with golden vineyards, fruit about ready for picking. This is the season of harvest tours, parties and weddings, plump burgundy grapes hang heavy. Harvest time is near and excitement fills the air.

After the crop is taken in, the full cycle has come near to an end, the vines cleaned off, cut back close to the vine, preparing for the harshness of winter. It is a time of rest. At every stage, the vineyards a continual reminder of God's work in our lives. Every season has its own beauty, and challenges, and divine purpose.

A vineyard is not a planting of one, but of many. The redeemed, all of us who make up the vineyard, are a reflection of the multifaceted wisdom of God. Thriving best in community, standing shoulder to shoulder, the life of the Vine pulsing through us, our branches weaving together as one

51

massive unit. Corporately, we are the vineyard of the Lord, stretching out, hill after hill, as far as the eye can see. God uses natural illustrations to illuminate spiritual truths. The lessons of the Vine and the branches are a perfect example.

The night before Passover, the festive nature of the evening was brought low as Jesus took off His outer garment, filled a vessel with water and proceeded to wash His disciple's feet. The Man in whom they believed was about to lower Himself to the position of a slave, the mood of celebration was redirected to a somber gesture of love, humility and sacrifice.

It was shocking, utterly, to the few who anticipated positions of leadership under the reign of their new earthly King, Messiah.   Under the fog of betrayal, denial, destruction and death, Jesus pressed in with preparation.

"Where I am going you cannot come," Jesus said. "Let not your heart be troubled", He reassured.

"I am going away but I will be coming back.   Arise and let us go from here."

A dark and eerie presence lingering, their hearts heavy with sorrow. By torchlight Jesus led His band of disciples into the darkness, destined for a garden.   Leading them through a vineyard, He sat down, the disciples knew what that meant. It was time for a lesson, another parable, and another mystery unveiled.   In the vineyard they pressed around Him to hear.

"I am the Vine," He proclaimed in hushed tone, the fire of torches aglow on their faces.

Who Am I

The principle of this parable, so critical to the life of a believer and to the Body of Christ, that Jesus saved it for this most profound moment. Earlier in the upper room celebrating the Passover supper, coming close together as family, Jesus took the bread, blessed it and broke it.

"This is My body, broken for you", He explained. Then He took the cup of wine saying, "This is my blood, shed for you," passed it on for each one to share. "Do this in remembrance of me."

Jesus had made it clear who He was and what He had come to do, and was now about to tell them who they were, not only they, in fact, but the countless number of us who would come after them. We are about to learn who we are.

"You are the branches", Jesus continued, "As I am in the Father, and He is in Me, so also I am in you and you are in Me."

As we abide in Him, and He is us, the supernatural result is fruit, the fruit of the Spirit, the fruit of righteousness, by the Holy Spirit thriving in us, the branches. We are the vineyard of the Lord, The Father ever tending, pruning and nurturing to impart spiritual fruit into a desperately hungry world.

Rest

"My Father is the Vinedresser," Jesus said.

Knowing how to bring forth the sweetest and finest fruit, the Vinedresser begins His work. Things that weigh us down, branches soiled by the world, unhealthy and damaged, He lifts up, gently cleans them off, gently pruning back unruly growth. The unfruitful ways in us are pruned off, helping us to be more fruitful. Likewise, branches that are heavy with fruit are trimmed back encouraging greater fruitfulness.

The bearing of fruit is the work of the Vine. The work of the branch is to rest and abide, staying close and drawing near. As we abide in the Vine, fruitfulness is the reward. Human nature pulls us toward self centeredness rather than self sacrifice. Sometimes, it is the attitudes of our heart that cause the most damage to the fruit, hindering the sweetness and flavor.

When our relationship with God becomes weak and broken, He calls us to return to our first love, alive with passion. He is the Fire, and as we draw close to Him, the fire is stirred in us again. The fruit of God's character becomes the life from which all other good fruit is born. The Love of God is the perfect fruit, His character flowing through us, revealed to us by Jesus and imparted in us by the Holy Spirit.

Not Alone

The indwelling presence of God in our life is the seal of God upon us for eternity. The "I in you and You in me" relationship that we have in Christ is dependent upon our willingness to abide in Him. Our purpose as a branch is to abide in the Vine, nothing more, nothing less, connecting, seeking after, drawing close. We cannot be partially attached for the life of the Vine to flow through us. We can work all we want, but if the power of the Holy Spirit is not flowing through us, there will be no fruit.

At times our own hard work will produce some results, but of little eternal value, and we will soon be drained of our own energy. It is about relationship. We serve out of the overflow of His power and life flowing through us. As the branch is abiding, living and receiving from the Vine, the power of God has uninterrupted flow, His immeasurable power toward us who believe.

As we abide in Christ, He does His work in us, righteousness, love and compassion for others is the response to Christ's character at work in us and through us. The world is desperate to see the genuine character and love of God shining forth from God's vineyard, as the branches let Him pour out His love to a world longing to comprehend the mystery.

"Abide in Me and I in you. As the branch cannot bear fruit of itself"

"He who abides in Me, and I in him, bears much fruit."

Living

There was a time when we had grape vines on our property. I enjoyed that time of year when the long branches needed to be pruned back to prepare for the next year's growth. The tender willowy branches never went to waste.

Taking one at a time, gently weaving them into garlands and wreaths, I could see the yet pliable limbs braided around to form beautiful decorations. After they dried thoroughly, artificial greenery, flowers and other adornments turned them into delightful pieces. I gave them away as gifts, displayed them in my home, hung them on doors and even sold a few. One thing they all had in common though. They were dead. No fruit or any other living thing could grow on those vines. They were only for looks.

It reminded me of stately old cathedrals with steeples and pillars and stained glass windows, looking beautiful, but often void of spiritual life. Society, and especially our younger generations are finished with lifeless sanctuaries that afford no answers, no truth and no vitality. They seek something real.

As the vineyard of the Lord, our only hope of reaching the generations is to be so intimately attached to the Power that the world will see good works and a love they can find nowhere else. Love is the fruit the world is looking for, an expression of the life of God in us that really cares. We must be the real thing to a world that is desperate for what only God can give.

Sweetness

Nothing is more distasteful than sour grapes, and so it is in the vineyard. Discontent, bickering and envy are sour grapes, our human nature rising up and working itself out in immature fruit. The unity of the Body of Christ is the most powerful agent on earth, and as we love one another and praying in one accord, no power on earth or in hell can stand against it. Could that be the reason behind such enemy bombardment, continually causing division and strife?

On the vine, it is often the new growth that must be trimmed back. Likewise, it is the new growth spiritually that causes pride. We have it all figured out, got the formula down, confident in our own ability and giftedness.

The Spirit and the Vine Dresser says, "No!". Take it back close to the Vine so the power and energy will flow to produce new fruit, better fruit.

As we abide in Him, and He in us, we will bear much fruit, and it will be sweet and enjoyable to others. The work here on earth is great, the needs overwhelming, far more than can humanly be accomplished. However, as we join our spiritual resources together, God is able to do far and above all that we can ask or dream.

About Love

To be the conduit of God's love requires that we first comprehend the vast treasures of God's love for us, as it becomes personal. God's love is not dependent on any goodness or perfection in our lives. His love is enduring and abiding, never ending, never fading. He loves us immeasurably, as largely as possible. Something that is already as large as it can get does not have room to grow. The only thing that can grow relative to God's love for us is our increasing revelation of its greatness. He loves us and nothing we can do will diminish its completeness.

Love is at the heart of every other spiritual fruit, and the truest evidence of His life in us. As the Father loved Jesus, Jesus loves us. Likewise, as Jesus loves us, our purpose is to pass on the love of God to others. By love others will know we are His disciples, connecting us to a world desperate to experience it for ourselves.

Jesus said, "All authority has been given to Me in heaven and earth. Therefore go and make disciples of all the nations, baptizing them in the name of the Father, Son and Holy Spirit."

This task will continue to occupy generations to come, but must be accomplished. As we share God's love with others, Jesus is lifted up around the world, the gospel changing lives and saving souls and the Father is glorified.

Joy

Can we know that our Heavenly Father loves us, blesses us beyond measure, and still lack the joy of it all? Yes we can. We believe it in our heads, but our hearts are sad, as one who is without hope.

"I will see you again and your hearts will rejoice and your joy no one can take from you," Jesus reassured.

Still, anguish of heart settled upon the disciples like a dark cloud of mourning. Then the sun arose over an empty tomb. They couldn't see it at first, but Mary did.

"He is alive," she cried, running as fast as she could. With the glorious announcement, fragrant scents of springtime filled the fresh air of dawn. Peter and John were the first to reach to vacant tomb, nothing but grave clothes lay folded and pressed, two angels sitting where the body had been.

"Who are you looking for," the angels inquired? "He has arisen, and is not here."

Joy was born that Easter morning, a joy that would change the hearts of mankind forever, a joy eternal that would sustain us through our darkest hours and calm our greatest fears. Our hearts are settled when we see the door of eternity approaching and He is waiting, His loving arms stretched out to embrace the homeward bound soul. Therein is found the jubilation that no one can take away.

Sacrifice

We have heard that one cannot choose your family, but you can choose your friends. "You are My friends," Jesus said.

Friendship implies a very personal relationship, based on respect and grace.   Yet, friendship in human terms can never convey the type of relationship that Jesus is describing.

We have friendships at many stages in our lives, some we call best friends, some who eventually we know as long time friends and old friends. Yet, no human friendship can begin to reach the level of love and unconditional quality that Jesus wants us to experience with Him, closer than a brother, the Word describes, closer even than two twins within a single womb.

"Greater love has no one than this, than to lay down one's life for his friends."

We are awakened to the revelation that Jesus is my personal friend, more devoted than any lover, and yes, I am willing to lay down my life for Him. We are called to become a living sacrifice, holy and acceptable to God, not as an act of martyrdom, but an act of love. My own needs become secondary to what nurtures growing relationship with Jesus. He is my Alpha and Omega, my beginning and end. In Him I live and move and have my being.

The Best

The call to love trumps all other commandments, and we cannot fake it. Apart from the Vine, we are but a dead stick. We can love as Christ loves only as we abide in Him, cling to and trusting His life in us, I in Him and He in me. As the life of the Vine flows through us, it is the proof of who we are.

How often we day dream, "if I won the lottery and had millions, this is what I would do…." Feed the hungry, build schools and hospitals, on and on we can imagine. Jesus chose us and appoints us to go bear fruit for Him. The value of a cup of water in Jesus name can have great eternal ramifications.

We don't need millions to affect the lives of hurting people, we need only the heart to do it, and as we step out in obedience to simply do what we can, giving our time, a hand, or a cup of soup, Jesus multiplies the act of kindness just as He did the loaves and fish.

Giving out of what we do have is the principle. The promise is that as we give from our meager resources, we can ask the Father for more, for whatever we need, and He will supply. When it comes to imparting His love and goodness toward others, we can let our visions be grand. Jesus says to ask the Father in His name for what we need, and that God will hear. There is no shortage of resources for the work God has called us to do. It is His promise, and it is as good as gold.

New Wine

The Kingdom of God is not in the raisin business. It is all about new wine. The process of making wine is very violent, for the fruit that is. The freshest, sweetest and mature fruit is crushed and pressed down, then run through a fine sieve.

The crushing of the fruit was accomplished in Jesus Himself. He was bruised for our us, becoming sin for us that we might become the righteousness of God. The New Wine of righteousness is the work of the Cross on our behalf, full of life, vitality and power. Then He sent us His Holy Spirit, to live in us, giving us the power to love and sweetness to accomplish the work here on earth, His life flowing through us by His Holy Spirit is the source and resource of every good work.

Christ in us, our Helper, is the Spirit of Truth who will teach us, and confirms the Life of Christ in us. The life of Jesus in us becomes as real to us as the blood pumping through our heart. He is the source of the peace and the joy of our salvation. He is our Hope eternal and our joyous anticipation.

It is Jesus in us who will fulfill the call of God to go, to become the new wine poured out. As we cooperate in rest and confidence that He is doing a good work, He is faithful to complete what He has begun, as naturally as breathing. Energy and readiness arise like the morning dawn. Striving will cease like rapids roaring over what appeared as boulders of impossibility before, the Life of God Himself is poured forth to the nations.

Lasting Fruit

Prayer is fruit that lasts. The prayers we send up today will multiply and affect the generations to come, lingering in the atmosphere of heaven for eternity, not like a morning fog that fades at noon day, but an eternal change in the atmosphere. God the Father always hears our prayers, whether in hush or audible tones, because He loves us, all of us.

Prayers offered in Jesus' name have a special pass through the gates, going straight to heaven's throne. The name of Jesus identifies us as His own, the power residing in relationship. At times when we know not how to pray, He knows the desires of our heart and hears every tear.

Why God has designed prayer to be in partnership with our participation is a mystery, but He knows, so we agree. Pressing forth in the power of Jesus name, prayer is the fruit that keeps giving and giving, conforming with His presence in us, the forces of heaven backing us with promise, sealed in covenant, and echoing through eternity, forever.

Who We Are

Worship is the sweetest of all fruit, as it is where we connect with God. It is our reasonable service, our response to who He is. Worship is expressed to God in as many ways as there are humans who have experienced Him.

God gave a diversity of gifts to all people, and as we use our giftedness and talents for His glory, it becomes our unique expression of worship. Found not in the act of doing, but in the spirit and attitude with which we do it, we worship in Spirit, expressed by His life in us, and in the Truth of who He is. The fruit of our creativity becomes the demonstration of our worship.

We are the planting of the Lord, a display of His beauty and splendor. Contemplating the goodness of God and His purposes in our service, be it a grand musical overture, a masterpiece of artwork, or simple acts of kindness and day to day labor in His name, that becomes our truest expression of worship, and in this the Father is glorified.

Our fruitfulness is the expression of who God created us to be. It is a reflection of His multifaceted wisdom and His manifold grace toward us. God the Father is concerned for exceedingly more than our individual destinies, but for our being a complete and corporate demonstration of His glory, His character to a world who longs to know Him, as revealed in the fullness of His Son, the Vine.

My Thoughts and Prayers

Teach us to Pray

From Luke Chapter 11

A Certain Place

First, by example, Jesus taught His disciples to pray. We see in gospel records that He went regularly to His certain place, always in communion, one with the Father in prayer. His disciples, observing, listening, watching, they wanted to know more.

"Lord, teach us to pray," they asked him, wanting what they observed in John the Baptist's disciples, true religious form and tradition. Still, they saw something different in how Jesus prayed, that is relationship. Jesus began with them, as He does with us all, right where they lived, in the open nature, not confined by temple walls.

Relationships are built upon communication, words and behavior. As the disciples watched, Jesus revealed the benefits of a "certain place." By instruction, He taught not as a ritual or a new tradition, but by conversation how to connect to the God of heaven.

Verse 1: Now it came to pass, as He was praying in a certain place, when He ceased, that one of His disciples said to Him, "Lord, teach us to pray, as John also taught his disciples."

Knowing Him

What is it about words? The fruit of our lips clearly reflect the state of our mind and soul. Words having great influence, will reinforce our own state of mind, and affect the thoughts of others, as well. Both careless words and words of affirmation are our witness, as faith comes by hearing. Our thoughts are where the enemy accuses us, bringing discouragement, destroying hope, so how we feed our thoughts and the thoughts of others is critically important.

Often, our prayers can begin with hopeless complaint, thinking only of our own hurts and troubles, effectively preparing the mind for sorrow rather than for victory. Therefore, Jesus taught the disciples, "when you pray, say...."

With positive mind and posture, we begin, "Our Father, who art in heaven, hallowed be Thy name."

We line up our own state with His, boldly entering the Throne Room of heaven, covered by the blood of the Lamb and the word our testimony.

Thou art God, Almighty Creator of heaven and earth, holy, righteous and merciful. I come as Your beloved child, Your son, Your Bride. Speaking audibly or in hushed tone, "My Father," we identify ourselves as His beloved. The doors of favor swing open wide.

Verse 2: So He said to them, "When you pray say, Our Father in heaven, hallowed be your name."

It is Not About You

What man believed to represent the Kingdom of God was power and authority, change and revolution. God saw His Kingdom on the earth through suffering and sacrifice. To comprehend Kingdom business, we must trust in God's sovereign will and purposes from His heavenly perspective.

"If anyone desires to come after Me," Jesus said, "let him deny himself and take up his cross daily and follow Me."

Often, we believe that our cross to bear is the accumulation of the trials and tribulations of our life. Truly, our lives do come with hardships, but they do not represent our cross to bear. Rather, it is our submission to the will of God, through it all, remaining faithfully focused on Jesus Christ, laying down our sense of deserving better, to follow Him. It is not about what we feel we deserve, but what God deserves, because of who He is.

As we set our hands to the plow, we move on from the hurts of our past and present, keeping our focus looking forward. Otherwise, as Jesus boldly announced, "we are not fit for the Kingdom of God."

In taking up our cross of faith and devotion to Jesus Christ through all situations, the purposes of God will be accomplished on earth as it is in heaven, to His ever increasing glory.

Verse 2: Your kingdom come.

Your will be done on earth as it is in heaven.

Daily

Jesus declared to His disciples while resting at the well Jacob built, "My food is to do the will of Him who sent me, and to finish His work."

Jesus was not ignoring His need for physical nourishment or denying that we all need daily sustenance. Rather, a higher lesson was on the menu for this day. Surrendering our will and plans to God, He will amply supply the opportunities to labor with Him in the fields of Kingdom work. Fields white unto harvest, fruit ripe for the reaping, we lift up our eyes and see. Pray to the Lord of the harvest to send more laborers into the field.

Souls as far as the eye can see, crying out for food in such a land of plenty, yet in a season of spiritual famine. Laying aside our baggage, we take up our tool box and follow Jesus. Everyday will present its own opportunities to serve, even in the seemingly small ways, just as Jesus simply spoke to the woman seeking water from the well.

Everywhere the seed has been sown there is work to be done, clearing thorns and rocks from the paths, preparing the way of the Lord. Some sow, some will water and some will reap, but all will receive the rewards as we share in God's finished work of the Kingdom here on the earth, feeding on His words of promise.

Verse 3: Give us day by day our daily bread.

Debt Free

The price of our sin has been paid. Fully comprehending our freedom, we extend that same pardon to others. We have no rights to hold on to the offense. We have no rights to withhold grace from another. The freedom from our own debt is more personally experienced as we set others free, all our debts being equal on God's scale of justice.

Our work here on earth is to set captives free, guiding others to the cross of forgiveness and unbinding the bands of the brokenhearted. It will require us to lose the guilt of our own offense as well, forgiving even ourselves.

Though it could be the hardest part of picking up our cross daily and following Him, nothing is impossible with God.

"Be ye kind to one another, tender hearted, forgiving one another as God in Christ has forgiven you." Ephesians 4:32.

Verse 4: And forgive us our sins, for we also forgive everyone who is indebted to us.

Watchful

Taking up our cross to follow Jesus onto the paths of service, we sometimes believe that our small and simple acts of service amount to nothing. Believing that we are not worthy of such a high purpose is part of the enemy's lie.

May every deceptive tactic be exposed by the truth of God's word, guiding our thoughts and understanding to what His word says about us, focusing on the truth not feelings.

When evil comes in like a flood, declaring lies discouragement, God raises up a standard against it to remind us who we are in His sight, the righteousness of God in Christ Jesus, blessed and highly favored. Promised by His word, if God be for us, who can stand against us?

Staying close to the heart of God, we are under the cover of His mighty wings of protection. Guarding our thoughts and walking in obedience to His word, our feet are secure on the path of safety. God is with us, and we need not be afraid.

"I will build my church and all the forces of hell will not prevail against her," Jesus says.

Verse 4 continued: "And do not lead us into temptation, but deliver us from the evil one."

The Prayer at Midnight

The work is pressing with new opportunities and increasing demands. Our human strength cannot carry us at the midnight hour, when we feel at our weakest. God understands. We were never meant to carry our cross by ourselves. Beyond our own capacity, we will end up burnt out, broken and humiliated, accept for the hope of Christ in us.

Jesus, ever alert to our faintest cry in the night says, "Ask of Me and see if I will not open the windows of heaven and pour forth more than you can contain, unto your bosom I will pour out."

Often our midnight prayers are our most desperate pleas. "Oh Lord, heal this disease, help me with these bills, save my child."

We can know that God hears our cry and stores our tears in a vial close to His heart. He sees from heavenly perspective and understands the deeper issues. For the lost sheep that is caught in a briar, the coin hidden in a dark place, a prodigal that has lost his way, God hears our desperate, twelfth hour prayer. However hopeless it may appear to us, nothing is impossible with God.

Verse 5: "Which of you shall have a friend and go to him at midnight and say to him, "Friend, lend me three loaves...."

Persistence

God does not play hide and seek, the stakes are too high for games, and our search for the real thing will not return void. He will respond speedily to the sincerely hungry.

Even our baby steps in search of God are seen and responded to as a loving Father would watch His beloved child make the efforts to balance. Our seeking after more and more of God is a lifelong, never ending response to knowing Him. The more we know, the more we desire, the more we seek, and the greater will be our awareness of His presence. He desires us exceedingly more than we are capable to desire Him back.

By revelation upon revelation God reveals Himself as the Lover of our soul. Stretching forth, knocking on the door of our hearts, He calls us to come close, to experience the heights and depths of His incomprehensible love toward us.

Verse 9: "So I say to you, ask, and it will be given to you; seek, and you will find; knock, and it will be opened to you. For, everyone who asks receives, and he who seeks finds and to him who knocks it will be opened."

Receive

Through miracles, signs and wonders, God shows Himself to us. By His still small voice, we have heard Him in their midst. The greatest sign of all, revealing the love of God and His righteousness, is the incarnation of His Son, Jesus Christ.

"If you have seen Me, you have seen the Father," Jesus proclaimed.

The cross of Calvary revealed His love, His power displayed at the resurrection. The same Holy Spirit that settled on Jesus' shoulder at His baptism is for us today. The Holy Spirit identifies the beloved children of God, working His wonders, speaking, healing and serving as Jesus did.

"In that day, " says the Lord God, "I will pour out My Spirit on all flesh," upon His sons and His daughters.

There is no magic formula to earn His promise. "Just ask," the Father said. How lavishly He will give upon the soul who simply asks. The Latter Rain, pours forth from the portals of heaven. Dreams, visions, signs and wonders will follow, streams of living water overflowing upon humanity. "Surely God is with us," will be our declaration, as whomever calls upon His name will be saved.

Vs 13: "If you being evil know how to give good gifts to your children, how much more will your heavenly Father give the Holy Spirit to those who ask."

My Thoughts and Prayers

Higher Ground

Reflections from

Luke, Chapter 6

New Wineskin

God's righteous heart is far more compassionate than our righteous standards, far more flexible than our rigid religiosity. His ways will override what we have come to accept as acceptable.

"A new law I give you," Jesus said. "Love the Lord your God with all your heart, with all your mind and with all your soul." "Love your neighbor as yourself," He adds.

"Who is my neighbor," the legal minds want to know? Even going against our doctrinal standards, the love of God trumps all. Our religious ways are as contrary to this new commandment as ever they were. Jesus never negated the call to keep the Sabbath holy. What He did, however, was challenge the question of what is holy.

"I am doing a new thing," Jesus says, "My ways higher than your ways, my thoughts higher than your thoughts."

Put away what you believed true before. Up is down and down is up. The law is replaced with grace, condemnation with kindness, judgment with mercy.

"Stretch out your hand unto Me, oh man," and you will be restored, revived, healed and saved.

Luke 6: 5: And He said to them, "The Son of Man is also Lord of the Sabbath."

Rags to Wealth

To fully comprehend the wealth of God's grace we must realize our own utter impoverished state without Him, entirely broken, beyond repair. Our life does not consist in the abundance of our stuff. We toil and labor from dawn to dusk and back again, building bigger garages to hold more cars, new accounts to store the overflow.

"You are fools," Jesus rightly spoke, "This night your soul is required of you."

Where our treasure is, our hearts are buried in the rubble. Laying down our wretched pauper's rags, putting off the old man of spiritual destitution, we can put on the new man, clothed in white garments washed in the precious blood of the Lamb.

May our eyes be bathed in salve to see our earthly state, with our Savior standing at the door of our hearts knocking, waiting for the invitation to come in and bestow on us an eternal inheritance no calculator can add.   "Silver and gold have we none," said Peter, "but such as I have I give unto you. Rise up and walk."

Luke 6:20, Then He lifted up His eyes toward His disciples, and said: "Blessed are you poor, for yours is the kingdom of God."

Luke 6:24, "But woe to you who are rich, for you have received your consolation."

Happy Meal

Oh, to be desperately hungry for truth. The truth of God's word stirs a desire for more and more, because its richness is beyond limits. Line upon life, precept upon precept, God's unfolding grace is revealed by the continual, never ending unfolding mystery. We are intended to comprehend the unlimited resources of God's treasures toward us.

We need not be satisfied with manmade concepts sprinkled with just enough truth to lure the seeking soul. Compromising truth will dim the light of the heart, causing our foot to slip into entrapments hiding in dark places. What we accept as our "personal truth", though sounding good, will only push us toward a pit of confusion.

"Return to the pure Word of God," He commands.

Incline your ear to Him and let Him answer the questions. He is always delighted to speak to a hungry soul and to connect the anchor points of truth. Let us hunger and thirst after God. He will supply from heaven, and provide spiritual nourishment, continually as fresh as the morning dew.

Luke 6: 21, "Blessed are you who hunger now,
for you shall be filled."
Luke 6: 25, "Woe to you who are full, for you shall hunger."

Oil of Joy

God has given us freedom to walk the path of our own choosing, even when the path leads to destruction. However, God is not lax as some would accuse Him to be, He is not blind.

The Son of God, with eyes like flames and feet of bronze, will not be shaken to compromise. Those who laugh in the face of God are fooling only themselves.

God's patience, nevertheless, is that of a loving Father. Repentance is a gift from God, evidence of His pursuit, as He reaches out for the one lost among the many.

"I came not for the righteous, but to bring the sinner to repentance," Jesus said.

The sincere sorrow for our moral decay will not be a matter of regret, but will lead to the perfecting of our soul. The Father will give us the morning star, and His mercies new every morning.

Luke 6:21, "Blessed are you who weep now,
for you shall laugh."
Luke 6: 25, "Woe to you who laugh now,
for you shall mourn and weep."

Counting

Standing for Christ comes with a cost. Salvation is by grace, a gift from God, but the forgiveness of our sin took a Savior, the Son of God being nailed to a cross, giving His life for the sake of ours.

"As men have hated Me, so also they will hate you," Jesus promised.

Those who call Jesus Lord will be as a fragrant aroma to some, and to others the stench of death, depending on which side of the Cross they stand. Persecution comes in many forms, and often the greatest demonstration of His presence in us is our willingness to stand regardless of the cost to us personally. Popularity with the world is a pursuit of folly.

Do we turn a blind eye in order to placate the powerful majority? Do we mind our own business when a neighbor is headed down the path of destruction? Our own churches can become so "seeker sensitive" that we hide our light under a basket as not to offend. World mission starts in our own home and neighborhoods, our towns and nation. Yes, there is a cost to pay.

Luke 6: 22, "Blessed are you when men hate you and revile you and cast your name as evil for the Son of Man's sake. "
Luke 6:26, "Woe to you when all men speak well of you, for so did their father to the false prophets."

Enduring

The law of love must prevail, even in the midst of injustice and prejudice. When they say all manner of evil against you, love them. When they beat you, throwing you in to prison, turn the other cheek. When they spitefully use you, don't repay evil with evil.

Most of us easily love those who love us back, but our challenge is to love in the face of hatred. When those whom we love reject the truth for the lie and hold us to account for their shame, we must remain steadfastly in love.

The new commandment is to love God with all our heart, mind, soul and strength, and to love our neighbor as our self. The challenge is to keep it in that order. Putting the call to serve God above the world is one thing, but it often starts at home.

"Remain in My love," Jesus says.

Stay generous, stay kind, stay hopeful. Your Father is merciful, and the reward great. You will be called the sons of the Most High.

Luke 6: 27-28, "Love your enemies, do good to those who hate you, bless those who curse you, and pray for those who spitefully use you."

Pass it On

We all deal with pride. It is both the state of a healthy mind, a means of survival, as well as part of our human nature. Pride must be tempered with meekness, which is strength under control. A balanced self respect comes from seeing our self as God sees us, of great worth.

Mutual respect and honor is seeing others as God sees them, looking past faults to love the person. God alone judges the character and the intentions of the heart. Forgiveness is not for condoning bad behavior, but being ready to release another from offense.

As God forgives us, we ought also to forgive others. The greater our willingness to release others, the greater freedom we experience ourselves. Our forgiveness of others is a response to what we have received. We are called to set the captives free.

Luke 6: 37-38, "Judge not, and you shall not be judged. Condemn not, and you shall not be condemned. Forgive and you will be forgiven. Give and it will be given to you; good measure, pressed down, shaken together and running over will be put into your bosom. For with the same measure that you use, it will be measured back to you."

Tenderness

How are we then to judge? You shall know them by their fruit. A lukewarm, half hearted devotion to Jesus Christ sickens God's heart. Believing they are enlightened, they are deceived.

Let the treasures of our heart reveal His love and mercy, careful not to draw our own conclusions. Sometimes, fruit is damaged from the heat of life's trials. Compassion will almost always reveal the true character of another and bring healing to life's brokenness.

It remains all about love and love is not harsh, it always thinks and hopes for the best in others. As people are loved, they can feel safe to respond to God's love. Jesus came not for the healthy, but for the sick, and that includes us all, there is no room for "self righteousness".

We all come to the cross with nothing to offer, our garments, soiled and stained. The righteousness of God in Christ Jesus is our only hope.

Luke 6: 43-45, "A good tree does not bear bad fruit, nor does a bad tree bear good fruit. For every tree is known by its own fruit. Men do not gather figs from thorns, nor do they gather grapes from a bramble bush. A good man out of the good treasure of his heart brings forth good; and an evil man out of the evil treasure of his heart brings forth evil."

Secure

Together, we are the house of God, built upon the revelation of Jesus Christ.

"Upon this Rock I will build My church," Jesus said, "and all the forces of hell will not prevail against it".

As the world feels increasingly out of control, we who are secured to the Solid Rock and will not be shaken, the sand and distractions of life swept away. The heat will be our friend, though for a season we may wonder what will come of us.

God has established great purpose for His house, the Body of Christ, with unity of purpose, united in prayer, and empowered with praise. There is no more powerful entity on the earth than the united Church.   Together we provide safety in the storms, accountability in times of temptation and strength through tribulation.

Jesus prayed that we would be one as He and the Father are one.   Through disillusionment and disappointment, many have separated themselves from the family, thinking that independently they will make it on their own. But, it was never meant to be so.

In our places of worship we come together to lift up the name of Jesus. Together we are a force to reckon with, whether our numbers be few or great, the power is the same.

As the Lord Jesus, the Lamb slain, the One who was pierced but lives, stands upon the Mount, we will stand with Him. The shaking will cease and peace will reign. We shall eat from the Tree of Life forever.

Luke 6: 46-48, "But why do you call Me "Lord, Lord," and not do the things which I say? Whoever comes to Me, and hears My sayings and does them, I will show you whom he is like: He is like a man building a house, who dug deep and laid the foundation on the rock. And when the flood arose, the stream beat vehemently against that house, and could not shake it, for it was founded on the Rock."

My Thoughts and Prayers

Wings

From Psalm 91

Warfare

When I grew up in the post World War II years of the 1950's, the consciousness of a nation who had fought the enemy in faraway lands was focused on safety at home. The "baby boomers", those of us born into this post war mentality, can remember clearly the sounds of air raid warnings, the piercing sirens blaring across peaceful blue skies, the experiences of "duck and cover" drills, forcing the innocent to hide under desks for protection. Oh, those images on the new twelve inch oval black and white picture TV tubes of fellow Americans building shelters in the back yard, stocked with supplies to last at least a week.

By the decade of the sixties, a "cold war" heating fiercely, the shocking reality was that the destructive forces of this world are far too ominous for our meager attempts of protection. In the threats of today's technological, science fiction-come reality world, we have come full circle to the realization that our fate is in God's hand.

He alone is our refuge, our provider, our hiding place. He alone is able and our confidence lies securely in Him. Will He do it? We are hard pressed to seek shelter in Him, and the promises of His word. He is our hope, He is Truth and He is able.

Shelter

There is a place, a place of refuge, a place of safety in the storm, a place of peace and rest, in spite of the turbulence of our times. In the secret chambers of God's holy presence sets the vault of His hiding place.

Jesus is the Way into the secret place of the Most High. Peace is found as our confidence rests upon Him. Our hope is realized as we set our minds on things above, knowing the love of God, His faithfulness and trusting the truth of His word.

God has spoken some radical things to us. Can we believe it? Our focus must be fixed on His enduring love for us, in spite of what we see with our eyes. Regardless of the trials and tribulations of this world, the truth is that God loves us and in Christ we abide in the secret chambers of His care.

The peace of knowing God's love brings a calm to our storm. Our Hiding Place, our Shelter and High Tower, we are securely tucked within the shadow of the Almighty.

Psalm 91: 1-2, "He who dwells in the secret place of the Most High shall abide under the shadow of the Almighty. I will say of the Lord, He is my refuge and my fortress. My God, in Him I trust."

Defense

The enemy of our soul, comes to steal, kill and destroy. No temptation has overtaken man, except such as is common. Yet, God is faithful and make a way of escape.

Our first line of defense is to stay close to Him, our eyes fixed on Him and His word. Christ is our victor. He has loosed the chains of bondage to the old nature, setting the captive free. As we stay vigilant, watchful and sober minded, the traps of the fowler's snare will be thwarted.

As a mother eagle sweeping down from the high cliffs, we are gathered up into the warmth of His wings. In safety and security, we will hear His voice, and He hears our cries.

The truth of His righteousness shall be our shield and protector. With vigilance, we are to be watchful and alert, and when the enemy rises against us, like a flood God raises His standard, and we will overcome.

Psalm 91: 3-4, "Surely He shall deliver you from the snare of the fowler, and from the perilous pestilence. He shall cover you with His feathers, and under His wings you shall take refuge. His truth shall be your shield and buckler."

Peace

Peace is not the mere absence of conflict or turmoil, but our place of rest in the midst of it. Our rest depends not on our circumstances, but in confidence that God sees, He knows and He cares.

We shall walk through the enemy's camp knowing the authority of the King as our backing. As trials press us closer to His bosom, the enemy's plots are exposed and defeated.

We need not be afraid of the wicked schemes by day or the fiery arrows by night, as hosts of angels are our rear guard and escorts through the valley of death's shadow.

Psalm 91: 5-6: "You shall not be afraid of the terror by night nor the arrow that flies by day; nor of the pestilence that walks in darkness, nor the destruction that lays waste at noonday."

Observation

Even when we feel overwhelmed by opposition, Lord Jesus, open our spiritual eyes. Help us to see the thousands upon thousands fighting the battle on our behalf. The hills are alive with chariots of angelic hosts, overseeing the affairs of the righteous.

The battle rages on in heavenly places, powers and principalities rendered helpless in the fallow of Your mighty hand. Outnumbered, the forces of evil fall by the wayside, thousands to the right and to the left. Our spirit eyes see the reward of the wicked, their utter defeat.

As if in a bunker of protection, we will observe the destruction of the lawless ones, thousands on every side, warring angels in our midst, fighting the battle of goodness, multitudes of heavenly hosts.

Can you hear the rattling of the sabers? It is always the sound of victory on behalf of our righteous God.

Psalm 91: 7-8," A thousand may fall at your right side, and ten thousand at your right hand, but it shall not come near you. Only with your eyes shall look and see the reward of the wicked."

Armor

We are hidden in God in Christ, our dwelling place, encased by the One who restrains evil. We wrestle not against flesh and blood and the weapons of our warfare are not earthly. Spiritual armor, for the pulling down of strongholds are positioned for our defense by God's hand.

The helmet of salvation, the Truth of Jesus Christ protects us from the deception. The shield of faith which will de-flame the arrows that fly at noon day. The breast plate of righteousness will guard our hearts, as we choose to draw close into God's safety zone. Feet prepared with the gospel of peace will guide our steps with wisdom.

Hidden in Christ, no man made attire, but mighty in Spirit, we are transformed into His power and glory.

Psalm 91: 9-10, "Because you have made the Lord, who is my refuge, even the Most High, your dwelling place, no evil shall befall you, nor shall any plague come near your dwelling.

Guardians

With ravines on every side, the straight and narrow way will keep our feet from slipping, being watchful to stay firmly on the path of righteousness, our place of safety. God's statutes are for our protection, our first line of defense, guarding our hearts and minds as well as our path.

Angels, countless in number, guard over the ways of the children of God. Watching diligently, they leading us away from the traps of temptation, able to step in at a flash to guard and guide us back to the Way, as we listen and follow the still small voice of Christ in us. The choice is ultimately ours.

Psalm 91: 11-12, "For He shall give His angels charge over you, to keep you in all your ways. In their hands they shall bear you up, lest you dash your foot against a stone."

Authority

The enemy roams to and fro like a lion seeking who he may devour. He is same old snake in the grass, deceived as much as he is a deceiver, up to the same old tricks.

God will make our enemies our footstool, the Word declares. It is about knowing who we are in Christ, filled with the fullness of the Godhead, an heir to the Kingdom, joint heir with Christ Himself. All authority He has been given, on earth and in heaven. He is our victory, He is our shield and protector. He is the Captain of our soul.

As we walk with Jesus, abiding in Him, we share in His authority. Our feet treading confidently through the maze of entrapments, and our victory is not by might, nor by power, but by His Spirit, our Commander and Chief.

Psalm 91:13, "You shall tread upon the lion and the cobra, the young lion and the serpent you shall trample under foot."

Favor

The eye of the Lord roams throughout the whole world that He might show His favor upon the one who is His.

Jesus, the author and finisher of our faith, He is our shield and defender, our High Tower, the Name that is above all names. In Him we live and move and have our being. He is the One to whom every knee shall bow, He is Lord.

It is by His favor that our destiny is played out, as God opens doors that no man can close, and bringing about divine connections, God's loving kindness and tender mercies following us all the days of our life.

He has set His love upon us. Grace and favor are our mantle, clothed in the robe of righteousness, the garment of praise. I am hidden in Him, My Deliverer.

Psalm 91: 14, "Because he has set his love upon Me, therefore I will deliver him. I will set him on high because he has known My name."

Our Hope

"A new covenant I will give" God said. "I will pour out My Spirit in those days."

The out pouring of the Holy Spirit, the Latter Rains, will refresh. Cleansing and healing will pour forth, and we shall know that God is in the midst of us.

The latter rains represent God's blessing both in the spiritual as well as the natural. Naturally, the early and latter rains upon the land are God's blessings, a reward for righteousness and obedience, insuring good crops in their season.

In the Spirit realm, the early rain, the grace of God prepares the seeker to receive the seed of the Gospel to take root and grow. The latter rains soften the soil and prepare it for the Harvest, by the work of the Holy Spirit.

From beginning to end, our hope is in Christ alone, to all who call upon His name.

Psalm 91: 15-16, "He shall call upon Me and I will answer him. I will be with him in trouble. I will deliver him and honor him. With long life I will satisfy him and show him My salvation."

My Thoughts and Prayers

Celebrate

Festivals

Miracles

The Great I AM

All About Jesus

From feasts of old to His I AM statements, miraculous acts of compassion, we see the Father's heart, revealed in Jesus Christ. It is all about Jesus who came to this world because the Father sent Him. The Father sent Him to reveal the truth, the multifaceted, manifold wisdom of God.

What is truth, we ask, in this post modern era? It is the same as it has ever been, that God loves us. Jesus came to show us the truth, that we are loved.

"I and the Father are One," He told us. "If you have seen Me, you have seen the Father." John 10:30

The truth is, that God so loved the world that He gave us His Son, so that who so ever believes on Him, shall have eternal life. John 3:16

The substance is Jesus Christ. The love of God made it all about Him, the Beloved Son, who is the Creator, the Revealer and the Restorer of all things.

Colossians 2:16: "The festivals are shadows of things to come, but the substance is Jesus."

Passover

Jesus, The Passover Lamb, His blood covering the doorposts of our hearts. "I AM the Way," He said, the true expression of God's love and His gift of Life eternal.   Jesus alone paid the price. He drank the cup of our iniquity, laying down His own life for ours, He alone was resurrected because of our justification.

By way of the Cross, The Way was secured, the Truth of God's love revealed, and eternal life bestowed upon all who will believe.

His first public miracle, He turned the water into wine, a gift of grace at the wedding celebration. As we put our trust in Him alone, we are also a new creation in Christ. The old is passed away and behold, all things become new. New Wine, the Life of Christ in us, is the miracle of our new birth in Him.

We join the celebration, as all of heaven rejoices. One soul at a time, the Father's plan is accomplished, the Truth of His unending love revealed in The Son.

John 14:6, "I am the Way, the Truth and the Life. No one comes to the Father except through Me."

Unleavened Bread

Jesus took the bread, gave thanks and broke it.

"This is My body broken for you", He said.

"I AM the Bread of Life." He is our unleavened bread, the sinless sacrifice, the Messiah of God. Bruised for our iniquity, the chastisement of our peace is upon Him.

As the five loaves multiplied to feed the five thousand, we see the grace of God is without limit. Unending numbers they come, multitudes in the valley of decision. One by one the bread is broken, "take and eat," Jesus offers. To as many as receive Him, to them He gives the power to become the children of God.

The search has ended, the Bread of Life is partaken. Still, the more we have of Jesus, the stronger our desire to know Him. The larger the vessel of our longing, the more and more it is filled. Without limits He supplies.

We need not wait for the end of our days here on earth to comprehend how measureless are His resources unto us who call Him Lord, our Bread of Life.

John 6:35, "I am the bread of life. He who comes to Me shall never hunger, and he who believes in Me shall never thirst."

First Fruits

Preparing the feasts and offerings of thanksgiving, the celebration of the harvest begins. Jesus Himself displayed the power of the first fruit.

"I AM the Resurrection and the Life," He declared.

As Lazarus lay dead in a tomb for days, loved ones stood helplessly weeping with broken hearts.

"Surely if You had been here My Lord," they mourned.

"Martha, do you believe?"

"Of course, at the end of days," her grief stricken heart responded.

"Jesus wept."

"Lazarus, come forth," echoed from the rocks.

So he did, wrapped in the grave clothes of death.

Jesus prepared our hearts to see the possible and to believe. Oh, what a celebration that will be.

John 11:25, "I am the resurrection and the life. He who believes in Me, though he may die, he shall live. And who ever lives and believes in Me shall never die."

Pentecost

Ascending unto heaven to the Father's right hand, Jesus promised to send back to earth a gift, the Holy Spirit, the gift of Himself.

"I AM the Vine," He told them, "and you are the branches", a picture of life ever flowing, imparting power and purpose. "You will bear much fruit because I go to the Father. Without Me you can do nothing," He added.

Nothing of eternal value, nothing of amazement that would open the eyes of the blind, set the captives free, or walk victoriously among the sea of lost souls, except for His life within. Jesus walked on the water, again demonstrating supernatural power.

"Greater things will you do," He promised.

The power of Pentecost is Christ in us. Do we have the faith to believe? Our eyes fixed on His, the life of the Vine flowing in and through us, is there anything to difficult for God?

John 15:1, "I am the Vine and you are the branches. He who abides in Me and I in them bears much fruit, without Me you can do nothing."

Trumpets

The trumpets sound, hailed with hope and glorious anticipation. Ages before the fulfillment, God clues us in to the mystery, a surprise ending, the new beginning.

I Corinthians 15:51-52, "Behold, I tell you a mystery. We shall not all sleep, but we shall be changed, in a moment, in the twinkling of an eye, at the last trumpet."

The gates of heaven will swing open, as the sound of the great ingathering begins. "I AM the Door," Jesus proclaims. No one comes to the Father but by Me.

As the thief unleashes his plots of death and destruction, a way of escape fills the heavens with great shouts of jubilation. The migration in a blink of an eye is accomplished, no one more joyous than the Father Himself.

The nobleman tasted such joy, his beloved child lingering at the doors of death. "Come Sir," even now at this late hour. Jesus heard his plea.

At the precise moment in time, the son escaped the grip of death's reach. So it will be for us when the trumpet blasts and we will lay down our works and traditions as filthy rags, and the Door of heaven opens , in the blink of an eye.

John 10:7, "I am the Door. If anyone enters by Me,
he will be saved."

Atonement

"There is no one to help me," bemoaned the man at the pool. "I cannot do it by myself," his cry.

Like him, our fate is hopeless without the extended hand of mercy. There is nothing we can or must do to "get there first", accept to grab hold of the Hand who saves us from our pitiful plight.

"I AM the Good Shepherd," Jesus declared. "I lay down My life for My sheep and they know My voice."

"Come unto Me," He calls out to all who have lost our way.

Nothing we can do will accomplish it on our own, so there is no reason to boast. The chastisement of us all was on Him, and by His stripes we are healed.

Jesus is our celebration of atonement, as we call upon His name, our pool of Living Water, and no one can snatch us out of His hand.

"Rise up and walk," we hear our Shepherd's voice.

John 10:11, "I am the Good Shepherd.. The Good Shepherd gives His life for the sheep."

Tabernacles

Like tabernacles, houses of worship, small and great, dot the landscape of this world. Far and wide, the church bells ring, the choruses sing.

"It is well, it is well with my soul," like lights in the darkness, reflecting the glory of Jesus, our anchor in the storm.

"I AM the Light of the world," He declared.

As Jesus spat on the ground then placing the warm clay on the blind man's eyes, he was healed.

"I once was blind, but now I see," the man shouted with joy.

Spiritual darkness is the most devastating bondage. Through the revelation of Jesus Christ, we are liberated from the oppressor. Our eyes are opened to understanding.

"Thou art the Christ, the Son of the Living God," said Peter.

"Man has not shown you this, Peter, but the Father in Heaven."

Upon this rock of revelation, the church is established. The Light has come, and we proclaim, "How great, how great is our God."

John 8:12, "I am the Light of the world. He who follows Me shall not walk in darkness, but have the Light of Life."

Eternal Flames

With eternal flames, candles in the wind, we celebrate God's inexhaustible supply.

"He is alive," the angels announced.

Our justification having been accomplished, death could not hold Jesus captive. The miracle of miracles happened that joyous morning, and we are insured life without end.

"I AM the Alpha and Omega," Jesus proclaimed.

It pleased the Father that, in Jesus, all the fullness of the Godhead dwells, and by Him all things are reconciled, both in heaven and on earth.

Jews and Gentiles alike, united as one new man, the Mystery of the Kingdom of God is revealed. From everlasting to everlasting, His mercy, the oil of our gladness, endures forever.

Revelation 1:8, " 'I am the Alpha and the Omega, the Beginning and the End,' says the Lord, who was and is and is to come, The Almighty. "

My Thoughts and Prayers

With Unveiled Face

A Love Song

Inspired by Song of Solomon

Breeze

A rustling in the trees, a fresh wind is stirring, an unsettledness in the atmosphere. I feel like I am being followed, a sense, a knowing, a desperation.

I am startled by a crunching of the underbrush, there it is, maybe, a breaking open of something that is about to happen and I will never be the same. An awakening in the deepest part of me is a hunger for God Himself.

Compelled by a longing knit tightly within me is the awareness that it is You , my Lord. Stepping lightly in the shadows.

Is what I perceive as my own desire for you, Oh God, actually the manifestation of Your longing and love for me?

Drawing

The unquenchable sense of Your presence presses me to earnestly seek You, to experience You. I stretch outward to reach, to grab hold, when suddenly I am acutely aware that I am the one who has been laid hold of. You have captured me, my Lord. It has been You pursuing me all along.

While I was yet a sinner, You gave Your life for me, my heart awakened to the revelation of You. Like a firefly, I am pulled into Your light, like a honey bee to the nectar of Your essence. The catch is Yours, my Lord.

Come, Lord Jesus, and meet the ever growing desire of my longing heart to experience Your presence in a deeper way. Draw me into Your ever increasing presence to know You. Satisfy this desperate ache in me.

This gnawing hunger in my soul, the embodiment of Your drawing me, my heart, my mind and my soul completely for Yourself. Is it possible that I could love You more than what You can love me back? I don't think so. You are indeed a jealous Lover, my Lord.

Price

How often I hold You at arm's length, in a mode of self protection. Why am I afraid of You, my Lord? Why do I allow You to approach only so far. Could it be that I don't feel worthy? Am I afraid of what Your love will cost me?

Break through to me, and don't let my own inhibitions stop Your pursuit. Let my slightest attempts to grab hold of You stir Your heart to apprehend me.   I hear Your still small voice, as I welcome You into this hidden place.

I am swept into Your presence, like being enveloped into the heart of a hurricane. My heart throbs for You, only to realize that it is Your heartbeat I hear. Your banner over me is love, and I cannot out love You, O Lord.

You sweep me to my knees in worship and an increasing awe. The fragrance of Your love is glorious and sweet. How can I resist You, Your all encompassing and obsessive love for me? I am undone.

Exposed

Lord God, am I willing to be so obviously identified? To be all consumed with Your presence within the secret chambers is one thing, but to be identified with You in public, am I willing? Would I print it on a T-shirt or post it on my blog?

A secret romance is never what You are after. It is Your love shed abroad in my heart that will touch a hurting world, giving food to the hungry, laying hands on the sick, telling others about You. That is the fruit of You in me. Am I willing? Yes. My answer is yes.

One encounter with Your presence does not satisfy. On the contrary, it drives me to a yet more passionate determination to seek You. To know You is to hunger in anguish for more and more. You are addictive, my Lord. I am hopelessly hooked.

It will only be a matter of time that I will be fully recognizable as "one of those people." Oh, to be recognized as one of those who know you intimately. May I be one that You see as Your eye roams to and fro throughout the whole earth, searching for the heart that is completely Yours.

Undone

Sacrifices and offerings will not earn Your pleasure. I cannot buy Your affection, my Lord, but a broken and contrite heart You will not ignore.

As I consider Your death, I am reminded of Your benefits on my behalf. I cannot proclaim Your death without a broken and contrite heart. No pride or arrogance can coexist with You there. It is not about how unworthy I am, but how gracious You are.

God, You are never far from me, but there are times when I don't sense Your presence. Do You withdraw from me at times? I don't believe so. Surely not.

Let me not grow so familiar with You that Your presence becomes a common thing to me. I thank You, O Lord, that You are always near, looking through the lattice, peering through the veil.

As I approach You with fresh desire, You capture me. It is again new to me, as with the first love.

Self

Help me to pull off the veil from my eyes and really see you. The veil of pride, independence and the sense of unworthiness must go. You are right before me. I willingly lay down every obstacle that hinders to lay hold of my destiny in you.

To my amazement, You are right there, and like Jacob I will proclaim, "God was with me all the time, and I knew it not."

Even in the pit of despair as I cry out, Your answer is always, always, "I am with you, don't be afraid."

Lord, let me never become so distracted by earthly cares that my eyes are blind. I want to see You in the midst of all life's challenges. Yes, You are there in the midst, right in the center, never leaving, never hiding.

God forbid that I should seek You half heartedly, lukewarmly, and think You are satisfied. Keep calling me out of my place of slumber and ease. Like a turtle dove in the evening midst, call forth to me, stir my heart that I will awaken to see You.

Breaking

You know me, Oh God, my innermost person. Thank you for seasons of flourishing, when the spring rains, the latter rains fall. Thank you for what seem to be seasons of dormancy, when life is still. The days of trial are realized as worth their weight in gold.

You truly are the only One who satisfies. I am like a flower at the end of the day, petals dropping. Yet, You are the heart of the flower, and at the twilight of the day, You are all of me that remains.

Your Love is all comforting, yet a sadness lingers. My heart longs for community, that loving bond of fellowship which seems like a fleeting reminder of yesterday. I am very aware that You are doing a sacred work in me, separating me unto Yourself.

You are revealing to me a treasure found only in the heart of the barren flower. It is You alone, my Lord, who can give me all that I desire, and I must learn that poignant truth to never be content with anything less. You are my heart's desire, You alone.

First Love

I pray, my Love, that the passion in my heart will not grow dim. My lamp was given ample supply. So, God forbid that I should leave home, taking the lamp with me, my "form of religion", and forget to take the oil of Your presence, for without You my lamp is dry indeed.

You have blessed me with everything I need for life and godliness, but I must be stirred up, fanned into flame. Please, let me never become content with less than a heart that burns for You.

Where, oh God, have we gone wrong. Your church has replaced Your manifest presence with feel good routines that won't transform our souls. Don't let us be satisfied with our man-made institutions and comfortable traditions. Create in us a desperate hunger for Your return. Unite us as again, full of Your power and love.

You said, "My Father's house is to be called a house of prayer."

We are hungry for You, Oh God. Pour out the Spirit of revelation and wisdom upon us. Woo us back to prayer. Help us to woo Your presence and power back into Your Church.

Fear

Lord, forgive me. My Spirit is willing, but the flesh is weak. I am more protective of my reputation than I am desperate for Your presence. I want to see and experience Your glory on my own terms, fearing what people think of me, I confess.

My desperation is overwhelmed by my propriety. I want the appearance of being full, while in reality I am poor, naked and hungry. Come to me, my Lord. My heart, mind and soul longs for the manifestation of Your presence and the demonstration of Your glory. Create in me a holy hunger for more of You above all else.

Help me to come into Your House prepared to offer my heart as a living sacrifice, focused on You only. You are there, waiting for me, so I come, help me to come near.

You are not hiding behind a darkened veil, as Your desire for me is more than I can desire You back. You await my out stretched hand, and as I seek You first, all the pressing needs are placed at Your feet. I approach You, my God, not with demands of my own, but to offer You my whole heart.

Beloved

Call me to the waiting place and help me to stay before Your face until I see You. My impatience beckons my imaginations to faraway places. Capture me, my Lord, hold my face in Your hands and call my name.

As I wait upon You, Your eye is on me. I cautiously step toward You and You see. You run to me as One who sees His beloved, coming up the dusty road, crossing over the grassy meadow. Seeing You afar off, I run to Your waiting arms. I am overwhelmed, my Lord , my Dear One. I am captivated once again.

Who am I, that You are mindful of me. Your embrace takes me to my knees to kiss Your feet and break open the precious oil of worship, my King. You have captured my longing heart. I am Yours, forever, everlasting to everlasting.

I am willing to be marked as "one of those", and with honor I carry Your brand upon me.   I will boldly and honorably carry the glow of Your presence into the dark places, the market places, the religious places. The veil has been lifted from my eyes, and as I gaze upon You, face to face, I am transformed into Your likeness, from glory to glory.

My Thoughts and Prayers

Then Sings My Soul

Psalms of Praise

Revealed

The glory of the Lord is meant to be understood. We are created to comprehend His greatness, as we look upon all of creation, seeing the demonstration of His handiwork, the earth and all of its beauty, intended to be the enduring revelation of the Living God.

He stretched out His hand and proclaimed, "let there be light", and the galaxies, moon and stars burst forth in all their radiance. Earth broke forth in fruitfulness and creatures of all kinds.

Although the tendency of man throughout the eons of time has been to focus on the splendor of the created, God the Creator was willing to take the risk, and all of creation reflects His Glory.

Psalm 75:1, We give thanks to You O God, we give thanks. For Your wondrous works declare that Your name is near.

Psalm 89:11, The heavens are Yours, the earth also is Yours; The world and all its fullness You have founded them.

The Plan

Through light years of time, angelic hosts proclaiming praise among the opulence of celestial wonders, God has always had a higher plan. As grand as earthly and heavenly treasures can be, the glory of creation is but a back drop.

"Let us make man in our image," they proclaimed. Male and female He created them, in His likeness He created them. Father, Son and Holy Spirit, standing in agreement, decreed that, "This is good."

The mystery of the Kingdom has never been about the dwelling place, but about the family. The lavishness of God left nothing lacking in His creation. The magnificence of God's craftsmanship was intended to delight us. From the most finite of creatures to the thunderous displays rolling across the prairie skies, God's handiwork is for our amazement.   Let my heart rejoice and join the angels chorus, "How great is our God in all the earth."

Psalm 7:17, I will praise the Lord according to His righteousness; and I will sing praise to the Name of the Lord.

Psalm 8:1, O Lord, our Lord, How excellent is Your name in all the earth, who has set Your glory above the heavens.

Good

The shortcomings of man have never taken the Creator by surprise. He formed us in the heart of heaven, foreknowing the ultimate price. The cross of Calvary was not a back-up plan, but at the heart of creation from the first yearnings of God's lonely heart. God counted the cost before He ever breathed life into man, and then declared, "It is good."

Though the sin of man broke the Father's heart, He countered it with promise, signed in the blood of the Son, and sealed by the Holy Spirit.

The covenant of reconciliation and the Seed of the woman were part and parcel in the plan of creation. God saw the beginning to the end, and still He declares, "It is vey good."

My heart and all my being declare the goodness of God. Let my soul cry out, yes to sing and shout, "Oh how great, how great is our God."

Psalm 8:3-4, When I consider Your heavens, the work of Your fingers, The moon and the stars which You have ordained, What is man that You are mindful of him.

Promises

That the Father would choose to enter into covenant with mankind is a mystery, except for His great love toward us. Knowing that man would make the deadly choice, to defile relationship. Though God clearly spelled it out, written on tablets of stone, man was a law breaking lot.

God Himself put the terms on the table, His longing heart determined to set the path of reconciliation.

"A New Covenant I will establish", He proclaims, with everlasting promise.

Who will pay the earnest for such an extravagant agreement? It would be His very own Son, the Prince of Heaven Himself, and whosoever receives Him, to them He gives power to become the children of God. Sending us the Holy Spirit, writing His laws upon our hearts, God will clean us as white as snow, from the inside out remembering our sins no more, and guiding us with Truth.

Psalm 103: 11 For as the heavens are high above the earth,
so great is His mercy toward those who fear Him;
Psalm 119:89, Forever, O Lord, Your word is settled in
heaven. Your faithfulness endures to all generations;

Glory

In the fullness of time, appointed from the very start, a star arose over a manger, the King of the ages laid wrapped swaddled upon the stable hay.

"Do not be afraid", the angels sang, "For unto you this day a Child is born."

King of Kings and Lord of Lords will be His name. He grew in wisdom and grace, born a man under the Law of Moses, to the tribe of Judah, heir to David's throne, the Seed of the woman's virgin womb. One with the Father and filled with the Holy Spirit, ears were opened, eyes could see and the dead saw another day.

"Are you the One who the prophets foretold?" they asked amidst the beatings. "I AM," He replied, as a Lamb led to His slaughter.

The skies grew dark at mid day, as the earth trembled and quaked. "Surely this is the Son of God," they said, the King of Glory stretched hanging on a wooden cross, broken for my iniquity, wounded for my transgression and by His stripes I am healed. Grace and mercy were born that day, a the sun arose upon an empty tomb. Death could hold Him there no longer.

Psalm 57:9, I will praise You, O Lord, among the peoples;
I will sing to You among the nations.

Victory

"Abide in Me", Jesus said, "and you will bear much fruit."

Christ in us, by His Holy Spirit, is our hope of glory, and He leads us on the path of righteousness for His name sake. I am no longer a slave to sin, my liberty was bought with a high price.

The call to holiness is a powerful mantle, and what God has commanded, He is able to do. The chains have been broken, I am free, free to walk in the counsel of His Word, free to resist the temptations of evil.

The devil is a defeated foe, and he has no rights. His accusations against us are null and void, we are a new creation in Christ Jesus. Old things are passed away.

Jesus became sin for us. He took it all to the cross and left it there, that we would become His righteousness, a demonstration of God's magnificent power. To God be the glory forever.

Psalm 24: 1 The earth is the Lord's and its fullness, The world and those who dwell there in; Psalm 29:2, Give unto the Lord the glory due to His name, worship the Lord in the beauty of holiness.

Asking

Life can be challenging. In fact, it is most of the time. Jesus comforts us in His declaration that He has overcome the world. The demands and hardships of life will serve to drive us closer to our source of strength.

Our victory rests in the lifting of our head, seeing above the challenges to the face of God, who is able and ready to help us through whatever life brings our way. The power of Jesus' name is our access to the inner chambers of God's provision.

Is that too difficult to believe that our heavenly Father so desires to bless and provide for us?

Where two or three are gathered, Jesus promises, He is there in our midst.

"Therefore, ask what so ever you will and the Father will hear," He said.

The power of agreement cannot be measured in earthly terms. It is beyond our comprehension, as true as Jesus Himself, my Fortress, my High Tower.

Psalm 61:1, Hear my cry O Lord; attend to my prayers. From the end of the earth I will cry to You. Psalm 121: 1-2, I will lift up my eyes to the hills. My help comes from the Lord who made the heaven and earth.

Power

Listening in on the courts of heaven, the sounds are unearthly, choruses of angelic voices joined with the great cloud of witnesses from ages past. Our hearts are beckoned to join in, and the waves of worship encircle the earth like a great tidal wave of glory. The Body of Christ bringing her joyful offerings.

The forces of darkness are shattered under the weight of its glory, wickedness bound by the power of praise. Armies have been defeated as God raises up a standard against them, with the dynamic of praise leading the assault. Nothing can stop it, a giant tsunami gloriously overtaking the wretched intentions of evil.

Let God arise and His enemies be scattered, the church marching arm in arm, our shields locked in agreement. God rides upon the waves, high and lifted up, the King of Glory is His name. "All hail His mighty power, is our declaration."

Psalm 95:1, O come let us sing to the Lord!
Let us shout joyfully to the Rock of our salvation.

Mercy

That God would so want to be in relationship with me, how can it be? Yet, it is true. Just as He walked the garden paths with Adam, God the Father desires a face to face encounter with us. When Adam broke covenant, the Father's heart was broken, even knowing the inevitability of it from the moment He breathed life into Adam.

We were created for relationship. The plan of redemption is all about relationship. God desired a people who would love Him by choice, not by program. The family of God we were destined to be, and through long suffering and great sacrifice, the Father pressed onward in love and determination. Jesus saw the ache in the Father's eyes.

"Not My will but Thine," was His response.

The love of God, how measureless, we sing. Oh, to know the height and depth of it all. We long with increasingly great desire to comprehend God's amazing love for us. We hunger and thirst to know it more.

Psalm 42: 1-2, As the deer pants for the water brooks, so pants my soul for You, O God. My soul thirst for God, the loving God.

Telling

"Go into all the world," Jesus commanded.

From the lowest valleys, to the highest peaks, God sent forth His call. Outpouring of latter rain has prepared the soil; rivers of life taking His presence to faraway places; the seed of His word is sewn into the highways and byways of all the earth. The fields are ripe unto harvest.

Prepare the way of the Lord. The laborers in the field are called out, the sickles of His Holy Spirit in their hands. Their feet shod with the gospel of peace, they are prepared. The storehouses of heaven are waiting, for the harvest of all the ages is at hand.

Dare to hear God's call upon your heart, the credentials of heavenly courts your backing. All authority has been given to the ones who are courageous to heed the prompting of God's voice. Make disciples in all the earth, baptizing them in the name of the Three-in-One God, Father, Son and Holy Spirit.

Some will plant, and some will water, but the increase is God's alone. It is time, we are prepared, and He is waiting. The vats will overflow and God will be glorified among all people.

Psalm 65:9, You visit the earth and water it; You greatly enrich it; The river of God is full of water; You provide their grain. Psalm 95:4-5, In His hand are the deep places of the earth, The heights of the hills are His also.

Behold

I looked up and saw a great city coming down from heaven, as a bride adorned for her bridegroom. There will be no night, and no need for a sun, because the King of Glory will shine like the noon day. There will be no more sorrow and He will wipe away every tear from their eyes. Nations will come bow at His throne, every tongue will confess that Jesus Christ is Lord. Oh praise Him who dwells on high, let our voices rise in triumph. The foe has been defeated and joy springs eternal.

Let them come from afar, just as they sought the Bethlehem star. Kings of all the ages will seek Him, Prince of Peace and Lord of Lords is His name. Sojourners from every corner of creation will come, through sky and sea and by foot they come, for better is one day in His presence than a thousand elsewhere.

The Kingdom of God starts here, it starts now. Set your heart on things above, because all that we see here will pass away. Yet, our hearts rejoice and in united voice we shout, "Come!" "Even so Lord Jesus, come!"

Psalm 72:17, His name shall endure forever; His name shall continue as long as the sun. And men shall be blessed in Him; All the nations shall call Him blessed.

Psalm 47:7-8, For God is the King of all the earth; Sing praises with understanding. God reigns over the nations; God sits on His holy throne.

My Thoughts and Prayers

Light

Together

Matthew 6:22-23

The lamp of the body is the eye. If therefore your eye is good, your whole body will be full of light. But, if your eye is bad, your whole body will be full of darkness.
Psalm 18:28

For You will light my lamp; The Lord my God will enlighten my darkness.

"I AM," Jesus said. "I am the way the truth and the light." When it comes to spiritual enlightenment, we cannot fake it. God alone knows if the light shining through us is the real deal. We are transparent before Him, and be it ever so dim, He promises that a "smoldering" wick, He will not snuff out. The transparency of our soul is the business of God. Our light is not hidden from Him, but neither are we to hide it from the world, or from each other. The Light of God in us is meant to be seen. As was John the Baptist, we are a witness to the Light of Jesus, that all may come to know Him. Jesus alone is the Light of the world, and all who follow Him shall not walk in darkness but have the light of life. The light passes from one to another and then another, as we are chosen to take the Light into a seeking world. God, the Father of Lights, has given us gifts and talents meant to be used to share with others. He has gifted each and every one of us, and together, we are the likeness of God, the Body of Christ. Our talents complement each other and tell of the wonderful creativity of God for service to one another and to the world, as we are reflections of His light, to guide others to the Source, God Himself.

Thrive

Isaiah 60:1

Arise, shine; For your light has come! And the glory of the Lord is risen upon you.

Psalm 27:1

The Lord is my light and my salvation. Whom shall I fear? The Lord is the strength of my life; Of whom shall I be afraid?

Yes, it is true, a deep darkness covers the earth and the people, but we need not be afraid. It feels so big, looks so dangerous. Shall we crawl back into our safe harbors and hide? We are told not to fear, for the Lord is with us. We are reminded not to despair, but to believe. Yes, the Lord will arise over us, each one of us who is willing to come out of our shadows of safety, where His glory will be seen upon us.

Find your voice, dust off your talents and cast off the fear. Our God is an awesome God. What are the gifts God has deposited in you. Stop, right there! Oh, yes you do have gifts the Kingdom needs for such a time as this. It does not have to be a scary thing. What are some simple things you have done over many years for your family, for your children? Cooking, knitting, sewing, crafts, the list is endless. Most of us are not delicate crystal lanterns, but the work horses. We carry the load, in the background of life, support ministries that make others look good, helping others to thrive. There seems, at times, to be no honor in the toil, but God's records are clear. His accounts tell the real story. Your mission field is the home and neighborhood where God has planted you.

Bloom there. Start with something which seems small in your own eyes, but enormous by Kingdom standards. The Father's heart whispers sweetly, "well done My love, well done."

Shine

Psalm 119:105

"Your word is a lamp to my feet and a light to my path."

Philippians 2:14-15

"Do all things without complaining and disputing, that you may become blameless and harmless, children of God without fault in the midst of a crooked generation, among whom you shine as lights in the world."

Has the Father left us in the world to make it on our own? You know the answer to that. For one thing, He left us His word, the light unto our path, a guide to our steps.

"Love one another as I have loved you," Jesus said.

Love, a timeless treasure apart from which no gift will shine, that is God's love, our hope. We imperfect vessels are only a reflection of the light within us. His strength is made perfect in our weakness, because it is the power of Christ which strengthens us.

Jesus became sin for our sake, that we might become the righteousness of God. It is all about Him, after all, not our own agendas or grievances, but for His glory we strive. Laying down our own rights, we take up our cross daily, and follow Him. For the sake of love, our love for Jesus and our love for others, we die daily so He may live. Walk as children of the light.

Power

Acts 1:8

"But you shall receive power when the Holy Spirit has come upon you; and you shall be witnesses to Me."

Romans 15:13

"Now may the God of hope fill you with all joy and peace in believing, that you may abound in hope by the power of the Holy Spirit."

Glorious, amazing, everything we need for life and godliness is ours, exceedingly, abundantly more than we can ask or dream, all by the Holy Spirit, Christ in us, our hope of glory. Paul prayed for us that the eyes of our understanding would be enlightened, that we may know the hope of His calling, the riches of His inheritance, the greatness of His power toward us who believe.

The working of His mighty power through us, so what's the catch? Too good to be true? To all who believe, that is the key. No tricks, no games. What would we do if we knew, rather believed, that all things are possible? What would be your wildest dream? That is a dream put there by your

Father in Heaven, bought by the precious blood of Jesus, and empowered by the Holy Spirit. Is there anything impossible with God? Really? Don't be afraid to dream, dream big. Step up, step out.

By prayer, example and service we touch the lives of many. From the privacy of our own homes, to the marketplace and beyond, we carry the light of truth. We shine in dark places, we change the atmosphere around our own cities to the ends of the earth. If one is so powerful a source of grace to the world, how much more powerful is our unity.

Together we are a city shining on a hilltop, a light on a distant shore. It presents a light so bright, so powerful, so glorious that it can be seen from space. The combined power of our prayers shake the world, overcomes disease and terror, sets cities on fire with revival. So powerful is the Church of the Living God that demons quake in our brightness.

"I will cause division and strife," the wretched one declares. "One spark of their tongue can set forests ablaze," he boasts.

"No!", will be our declaration. "They will know us by our love!"

Taking the light, arm in arm we march forward. We can do this. With the power of God in us, we can put aside our differences and fix our eyes on His higher purposes. Walls will fall, deaf will hear, blind will see. Springs of Living Water will flow in the desert places, and then all who call upon the name of the Lord will be saved.

Watch

John 8:12

"Then Jesus spoke to them again saying, "I am the light of the world. He who follows me shall not walk in darkness."

I Thessalonians 5:5-6

"You are all sons of light and sons of the day. We are not of the night nor of darkness. Therefore let us not sleep as other do, but let us watch and be sober."

As Jesus is our Light, we are to be the light in the darkness on the shores of rocky seas. Someone is looking, trying to find their way, so be alert and watchful. It might be right off the coast of our own household. We are a chosen generation, a royal priesthood, called out into His marvelous light, to His glory and praise, with influence and authority. Watch, pray and declaring over the next generation. Like with the faithful of old, "they saw from afar off," even if it did not come to pass in their own life times.

As grandparents, we see from afar off, and we are compelled to cry out to the Lord, "Oh God, pour out upon them the revelation of Jesus Christ, that they know You, the Son of the Living God."   Not by intellectual assent but by the Spirit of God. Their ordained purposes are empowered by the knowledge of God. The "scarlet cord" in their generation presses forward into the next, and then the next.

The word legacy comes strongly to mind. What can I leave behind? Nothing can take the place of time and relationship, yet the sense of legacy is our desire for their sake. The priestly prayer of blessing over them, the pronouncement of God's love, the proclamation of His intentions are declared for God's perfect time. With the show of love and acceptance of who God created them to be, patiently we wait upon His hand, the One who loves them exceedingly more than we are able, nothing is impossible.

Watch and pray it through for as long as we have breath to breathe. Showing God's love, quietly observing the trials that come their way, we know that God is working His goodness, conforming them to His likeness, and our heart is grateful for the privilege of being Grandma, especially on those occasions when they call and say, "Grandma, please pray."

Faithful

Revelation 22:4-5

"*They shall see His face, and His name shall be on their foreheads. There shall be no night there: They need no lamp nor light of the sun, for the Lord God gives them light. And they shall reign forever and ever.*"

"Well done my faithful servants," will be God's declaration. "Come enter your rest."

In Heaven, our greatest reward will be the presence of the Living God, but the presence of our children with us must be a close runner up. His coming draws close, closer every waking day. We are to encourage one another with that hope. We will overcome by the words of our testimonies, our stories of victory, and united by the blood of the Lamb.

Through hills and valleys we have come, standing shoulder to shoulder, marching to the gates of victory. We see His appearing, like brides-to- be, our lamps trimmed and filled, we see Him face to face. The marriage supper of the Lamb is here.

Dressed in sparkling robes, we hear His call, "Come away My beloved."

Oh, what a glorious day, anticipated with all joy and praise. Don't give up the fight. Boldly declare from the housetops, "The King is Coming."

We all have our parts to play, small and large, we do what God has blessed us to do. We write, we paint, we teach, we pray. Through whatever gifts and talents God has bestowed, we must be about our Father's business. Nothing is too grand or humble in God's economy. Whatever means He has provided for us personally and collectively, we purposefully use for His glory.

Well done, indeed!

My Thoughts and Prayers

Additional Copies Available at:

https://www.createspace.com/3712217

Made in the USA
San Bernardino, CA
02 July 2016